THE AUTHOR ASSUMES, BY ONE'S PERUSAL OF THIS VOLUME, THAT ONE IS IN DIRE NEED OF ASSISTANCE.

STYLE & CIRCUMSTANCE

THE GENTLEPERSON'S

Guide to

GOOD GRAMMAR

THE AUTHOR shall offer enlightenment regarding how best to overcome one's vexation with the English language and learn to avoid the most common mistakes.

HEED, HOWEVER, THESE WORDS: THIS BOOK IS A GUIDE FOR **GENTLEPERSONS**; THAT IS TO SAY, THOSE WHO WOULD NOT FLAUNT THEIR SYNTAX BOASTFULLY, BUT RATHER, LET THEIR WELL-STRUCTURED AND GRAMMATICALLY CORRECT SENTENCES SPEAK FOR THEMSELVES.

PHINEAS J. CARUTHERS

Adamsmedia
Avon, Massachusetts

Published by
Adams Media, a division of F+W Media, Inc.
57 Littlefield Street, Avon, MA 02322. U.S.A.
www.adamsmedia.com

Contains material adapted and abridged from *The Only Grammar
Book You'll Ever Need*, by Susan Thurman, copyright © 2003 by
F+W Media, Inc., ISBN 10: 1-58062-855-9, ISBN 13: 978-1-58062-
855-6 and from *101 Things You Didn't Know about Jane Austen: The
Truth about the World's Most Intriguing Romantic Literary Heroine*, by
Patrice Hannon, PhD, copyright © 2007 by F+W Media, Inc., ISBN
10: 1-59869-284-4, ISBN 13: 978-1-59869-284-6.

ISBN 10: 1-4405-3062-9
ISBN 13: 978-1-4405-3062-3
eISBN 10: 1-4405-3118-8
eISBN 13: 978-1-4405-3118-7

Printed in the United States of America.

10   9   8   7   6   5   4   3   2   1

Library of Congress Cataloging-in-Publication Data
is available from the publisher.

*This book is available at quantity discounts for bulk purchases.
For information, please call 1-800-289-0963.*

CONTENTS

CHAPTER 7
WRITING BETTER SENTENCES — 165

CHAPTER 8
AVOIDING COMMON ERRORS — 187

To
His Royal Highness
The Prince Regent,
This Work Is,
By His Highness's Permission,
Most Respectfully Dedicated,
By His Royal Highness's
Dutiful
And Obedient
Humble Servant
THE AUTHOR

INTRODUCTION

W elcome, dear reader. The Author assumes that one's perusal of this volume indicates that one is in dire need of assistance and not that one is spitefully flipping through the pages in hopes of finding an error.

If the former, fear not: The Author shall offer enlightenment regarding how best to overcome one's vexation with the English language and learn to avoid the most common mistakes. If the latter, should one succeed in finding any errata, please direct one's missives to The Editor, as it is not The Author's fault.

The wisdom contained within these pages shall bestow upon the one who reads it the ability to communicate gracefully and appropriately, thus making one more likely to correct another person's speech or writing as be, oneself, corrected. An agreeable prospect, one must concede.

Heed, however, these words: This book is a guide for *gentlepersons*; that is to say, those who would not flaunt their syntax boastfully, but rather, let their well-structured and grammatically correct sentences speak for themselves. Dear reader, it is better to be modestly silent and know that one is superior to all others in the room than to gabble on and on about it.

One with a masterful grasp of the language and its uses will reveal one's superiority as soon as one speaks. Others will admire one. Perhaps they will ask where one learned to use one's pronouns so effectively, or how they can learn the difference between *who* and *whom*. In reply, The Author hopes one will produce this tome and offer it up to the asker before proceeding to the nearest stationer's to procure another copy.

CHAPTER 1
FINDING THE RIGHT WORDS

T hose who are mean in understanding oft communicate it in their choice of words. If one wishes to impress others with one's erudite ways, one must be certain to select the appropriate word to use in the appropriate place. If one wishes not to miscommunicate, then one must also spell the appropriate word appropriately!

If one wishes to lose the attention of one's reader, then by all means one may throw together words in any slapdash manner. Even better—care not a farthing for the correct spelling, and add capital letters at whim! That will ensure that one's readers snort contemptuously and toss aside one's work.

Herewith are the most basic rules of English spelling and the most commonly misused and confused words.

Spelling It Out

If one has received any proper education, then one has heard this rhyme:

> ❧ I *before* e,
> *Except after* c,
> *Or when sounded as* a,
> *As in* neighbor *or* weigh.

While said rhyme is a cringeworthy example of school-room doggerel, it does in fact convey the correct approach to spelling such words as *ceiling, conceive, feign, field, inveigh, obeisance, receive, shield, sleigh,* and *weight.*

But this rule fails to take into consideration such words as *ancient, being, conscience, efficient, either, feisty, foreign, height, kaleidoscope, leisure, nonpareil, protein, reimburse, science, seize, society, sovereign, species, sufficient,* and *weird.*

Consider this one's first lesson in the art of writing: All rules have exceptions and must be considered as guidelines only. Additionally, if one were to invest in the acquisition of a dictionary, one's efforts to spell words correctly would be greatly aided.

Now, let us consider the act of multiplication—as it applies to writing. (The Author hopes one did not infer a different act of multiplication.) Herewith, we will delve into the mysteries of turning one item into two or more.

Forming Plurals of Nouns

1. To form the plural of most English words that do not end in *−s*, *−z*, *−x*, *−sh*, *−ch*, or *−ss*, add *−s* at the end:

   ✑ *desk = desks, carriage = carriages, book = books*

2. To form the plural of most English words that end in *−s*, *−z*, *−x*, *−sh*, *−ch*, and *−ss*, add *−es* at the end:

   ✑ *Michaelmas = Michaelmases, box = boxes, dish = dishes, church = churches, loss = losses*

   There exist some exceptions to this rule (pray tell, when do they not?). Such exceptions include *quizzes, frizzes,* and *whizzes.* (Note, dear reader, that the *−z* is doubled.) However, one would not use such terms in polite society anyway.

3. To form the plural of some English words that end in *−o*, add *−es* at the end:

   ✑ *potato = potatoes, echo = echoes, hero = heroes*

   Note, however, the aforementioned disclaimer: "some English words." For *other* English words that end in *−o*, add only *−s* at the end:

❧ *inferno = infernos, alto = altos, two = twos, piano = pianos, solo = solos*

Additionally—just to make one pull one's mustache hairs out by the roots—some words ending in *–o* can form the plural in either way:

❧ *buffalo = buffaloes/buffalos, cargo = cargoes/cargos*

When in doubt about which form to use, a gentleperson will consult the dictionary and use the plural form that is listed first.

4. To form the plural of most English words that end in a consonant plus *–y*, change the *y* to *i* and add *–es:*

❧ *lady = ladies, candy = candies, penny = pennies, prosody = prosodies*

5. To form the plural of most English words that end in a vowel plus *–y*, add *–s:*

❧ *joy = joys, Monday = Mondays, key = keys, attorney = attorneys, bailey = baileys*

6. To form the plural of most English words that end in *–f* or *–fe*, change the *f* to *v* and add *–es:*

❧ *knife = knives, leaf = leaves, wife = wives, wolf = wolves*

Some exceptions to this rule exist. One may have an *oaf* for a brother-in-law, but one would not have *oaves*. One would have *oafs*. That is, one would simply add *–s* to form the plural. The same is true of *chef* and *chief.*

Do note that most words ending with an *–ff* simply add *–s* to form their plural:

❧ *cliff = cliffs, tariff = tariffs, bailiff = bailiffs*

7. Some words form their plurals in ways that defy useful categorization; these are ancient words that made their way into the language before grammarians could neaten them up:

🖎 *child = children, mouse = mice, foot = feet, person = people, tooth = teeth, ox = oxen*

8. Foreign words, such as those of Greek or Latin origin, often have an irregular plural. In some cases, both the regular and irregular plural forms are acceptable. Of course, to subtly flaunt one's education, one should use the irregular form, scoffing at the regular form as useful only for the uneducated masses. (Unless one is in the hideous circumstance of having an employer who insists otherwise. Then one must do what one must do.)

alumnus	alumni
analysis	analyses
radius	radiuses or radii
focus	focuses or foci
fungus	funguses or fungi
index	indexes or indices

9. If one wishes not to make a misstep, one must also maintain vigilance in matters concerning words that are the same in both singular and plural forms:

🖎 *deer, offspring, crossroads, headquarters, fish, series*

The pain The Author feels upon hearing a usage such as "Look at all the deers!" is quite unsupportable.

Adding Prefixes and Suffixes

Sometimes the meaning of a word is altered by adding a beginning or an ending to it. A prefix is such an alteration that occurs at the beginning of a word:

❧ *think* ➤ *rethink*

Perhaps one has hastily sent an ill-conceived missive to a lady of one's acquaintance. One might wish to disavow it. Thus, one might say, "Please *dis*regard my letter of 3 January 1838. Imagine my *dis*comfort and *un*ease when I learned the footman had taken a leaf from a novel I am writing and sent it to you." In these instances, the prefixes serve to indicate the opposite of the word they are attached to:

❧ *regard* ➤ *disregard (do not regard)*
❧ *comfort* ➤ *discomfort (not comfort)*
❧ *ease* ➤ *unease (not ease)*

When such an alteration occurs at the end of a word, it is called a suffix:

❧ *consider* ➤ *considerable*

1. Words that end in −*x* do not change when a suffix is added to them:

❧ *vex = vexing, hoax = hoaxed, mix = mixer*

2. Words that end in −*c* do not change when a suffix is added to them if the letter before the *c* is *a*, *o*, *u*, or a consonant:

❧ *talc = talcum, maniac = maniacal*

3. Words that end in −*c* usually add *k* when a suffix is added to them if the letter before the *c* is *e* or *i* and the pronunciation of the *c* is hard:

❧ *picnic = picnickers, colic = colicky, frolic = frolicking*

4. Words that end in −*c* usually do not change when a suffix is added to them if the letter before the *c* is *e* or *i* and the pronunciation of the *c* is soft:

❧ *critic = criticism, clinic = clinician, lyric = lyricist*

5. Words that end in a single consonant that is immediately preceded by one or more unstressed vowels usually remain unchanged before any suffix:

❧ *debit = debited, credit = creditor, felon = felony, travel = traveled, label = labeling*

Now, dear reader, one must know that an exception is to be expected. And, without further ado, here it is. In some cases, the final letter is doubled before the suffix is added:

❧ *program = programmed, format = formatting, crystal = crystallize*

6. When a prefix is added to form a new word, the root word usually remains unchanged:

❧ *spell = misspell, cast = recast, approve = disapprove*

In some cases, however, one must add a hyphen to the new word thus resulting. These exceptions include when the last letter of the prefix and the first letter of the word it is joining are the same vowel:

❧ *re-enter*

When the prefix is being added to a proper noun:

❧ *mid-March*

And when the new word formed by the prefix and the root must be distinguished from another word spelled in the same way but with a different meaning:

🖎 *re-creation (versus recreation)*

7. When adding a suffix to a word ending in *–y*, change the *y* to *i* when the *y* is preceded by a consonant:

🖎 *carry = carrier, irony = ironic, empty = emptied*

Note that this rule does not apply to words when an *–ing* ending is added:

🖎 *carry = carrying, empty = emptying*

This rule also does not apply to words in which the *–y* is preceded by a vowel:

🖎 *delay = delayed, enjoy = enjoyable*

8. Two or more words that join to form a compound word usually keep the original spelling of each word:

🖎 *cufflink (cuff + link), billfold (bill + fold), bookcase (book + case), footman (foot + man), charwoman (char + woman), fishwife (fish + wife)*

9. If a word ends in *–ie*, change the *–ie* to *–y* before adding *–ing*:

🖎 *die = dying, lie = lying, tie = tying*

10. The correct spelling of the suffix meaning "full of" is *–ful*:

🖎 *armful, deceitful, baneful, bountiful, useful, colorful*

Helpful Spelling Devices

If one has reached this point in the narrative fully convinced that there exist more exceptions to the rule than otherwise, one would not be alone. However, one must not give in to defeat and despair; one must find another way!

Some individuals, The Author included, use assistive devices, such as the rhyme at the beginning of this chapter, to aid memory. (One must also remember that there is no shame in keeping a dictionary at one's elbow; indeed, it can serve as a silent symbol to visitors of one's intellectual prowess.)

Listed herewith are some commonly misspelled words and suggested devices to help one remember the correct spelling.

arctic: The first *c* is often omitted when writers attempt to celebrate the achievements of noble explorers such as Sir John Franklin. Remember the first letter of each word of this sentence: "*A R*eally *C*old *T*ime *I*s *C*oming."

business: The first part of the word is oft misspelled. Remember: "I often take the *bus* in my business."

cemetery: All of the vowels are *e*s. Remember: "*E*pitaphs are found in a cemetery."

dilemma: One *m* or two? Remember: "*E*mma faced a dilemma."

exceed: Is it spelled *–eed* or *–ede?* Remember: "Do not exceed a safe sp*ee*d."

February: Even though the word is commonly mispronounced, there is an *r* after the *b*. Remember: "*Brr*, it is cold in February."

grammar: This word is spelled with an *–ar* on the end. Remember: "Bad grammar will *mar* one's chances for acceptance among the elite."

knowledge: Spellers often omit the *d*. Remember: "That le*d*ge is dangerous."

loneliness: The first *e* is often omitted. Remember: "The *lone* wolf is known for his loneliness."

marriage: Is it *–aige* or *–iage?* Remember: "One must be a certain *age* for marriage."

parallel: Is it *–allel* or *–alel?* Remember: "There are two para*ll*el lines in the middle of parallel."

rhythm: The two *h*s usually pose the problem. Remember: "Two syllables, two *h*s."

roommate: This is often misspelled with only one *m*. Remember: "Two roommates, two *m*s."

separate: The word is often misspelled by writing the second vowel as an *e*. Remember: "There is *a rat* in separate."

Commonly Confused Words

If one is not sure whether one needs *advice* or *advise* about distinguishing *between* (or is that *among?*) words that frequently cause confusion, then one will find something of benefit in studying the following section. It contains an extensive list of words that are commonly confused or misused, along with—if The Author may be so bold—an exceptionally clear explanation of when each should be used.

a, an: *A* is used before words that begin with a consonant sound (*a* pig; *a* bumposopher; *a* knave); *an* is used before words that begin with a vowel sound (*an* academic, *an* ancestor). The sound is what makes the difference. Write *a habit* because *habit* starts with the *h* sound after the article, but write *an honor* because the *h* in *honor* isn't pronounced (the first sound of *honor* is the vowel *o*).

> ❧ *What an honor and a privilege it is to meet a history expert such as Mrs. Thorndyke.*

a lot, alot, allot: If one has had more than an iota of education, then one knows that *alot* is not a word and one may skip the next several sentences. If one means to indicate a great number of people, use *a lot*. No, wait, please do not use the phrase at all. Choose instead a more befitting word or phrase: "many" or "a great number." If one means *to allocate*, use *allot*. A memory device for *allot* is *allocate = allot*.

> ❧ *Tomorrow night, the queen will allot a lot* of money for various municipal projects.*

*Example included only under duress. If one wishes to convey one's humbling lack of education, then by all means continue to use "a lot" in writing and in conversation.

accept, except: *Accept* has several meanings, including *believe, take on, endure,* and *consent; except* means *excluding*. If one's sentence can keep its meaning if one substitutes *excluding*, use *except*.

> ❧ *Everyone except the pope is expected to accept the invitation to attend Queen Elizabeth's Golden Jubilee.*

adapt, adopt: To adapt is to change; to adopt is to take and make one's own.

> ❧ *After Victoria adopted a cat, Albert adapted to getting clawed.*

adverse, averse: *Adverse* means *unfavorable* or *unpleasant*; *averse* means *reluctant*. A memory device is to picture people who do not care to speak before a group; if they were called upon to recite a poem, they would be *averse* to reciting *a verse*. As all gentlepersons in polite society should be.

advice, advise: *Advise* is what one does when one gives *advice*. Herewith, a memory device to help one remember: To adv*ise* one must be w*ise*. Good adv*ice* is to walk slowly on *ice*.

❧ *My schoolmaster tried to advise me when I was a young-ster, but I failed to heed his advice.*

affect, effect: *Affect* is usually a verb (something that shows action), usually means *change* or *shape*, and—as a verb—has its accent on the second syllable. *Effect* is almost always a noun meaning *result* or *outcome, appearance* or *impression*. (*Effect* has a rare use as a verb, when it means *to achieve* or *cause*.)

❧ *The effect of the announcement of the Poor Law Amend-ment Act will do nothing to affect poor Adam's term in the workhouse. To effect his escape, he will need a conspirator.*

aggravate, annoy: If one means to *pester* or *irritate*, one wants to *annoy*. *Aggravate* means *exaggerate* or *make worse*.

❧ *Mrs. Bennet was annoyed when Mr. Bennet aggra-vated the condition of her nerves by refusing to visit Netherfield.*

aid, aide: If one helps others, one is said to *aid* them; if one has a help*er* or support*er* (such as a private secretary or a valet), one has an aid*e*.

❧ *The aid from one's aide is invaluable.*

aisle, isle, I'll: An *aisle* is a passageway in a theater, church, or other building; an *isle* is an island (a shortened form of the word); *I'll* is short for *I will.*

❧ *Lizzie will walk down the aisle to meet her bridegroom; then they will honeymoon on a desert isle and I'll wish them bon voyage.*

all ready, already: If one means that all is ready, one must use *all ready*; if one means that something has occurred in the past, use *already.*

❧ *Victoria was already queen when she was finally all ready to marry Albert.*

all right, alright: One often flinches to see the incorrect spelling *alright*; *all right* is always two words. One would not say something is *alwrong*, would one? (The very idea brings The Author very near tears!)

❧ *It is all right to eat with one's fingers—if one is two years old!*

all together, altogether: *All together* means *simultaneously* or *all at once*; *altogether* means *entirely* or *wholly*. If one can substitute *entirely* or *wholly* in the sentence and the meaning does not change, one needs the form of the word that is entirely, wholly one word.

❧ *Mr. Darcy is altogether wrong about the six friends going all together to church; each is going separately.*

allowed, aloud: If one means *out loud* (as in *audible*), use *aloud*; if one means one has permission, use *allowed.*

❧ *During the prayer, one is not allowed to speak aloud.*

alumni, alumnae, alumnus, alumna: One can thank the Romans for this perplexing mass of confusion; Latin has separate words for masculine, feminine, singular, and plural forms of nouns. One male graduate is an *alumnus*; one female graduate is an *alumna*; several female graduates are *alumnae*; and several male graduates or several male and female graduates are *alumni*. One can see why the short form *alum* is often used informally; it is easier than looking up the correct form. But a gentleperson will always reach for the dictionary rather than be accused of lazy writing.

> ❧ *Although Josephine and her sisters are alumnae from Bridgnorth, Josephine is the alumna who receives the most attention; her brothers Martin and Xavier are alumni of Eton, but Martin is a more famous alumnus than Xavier.*

allusion, illusion: An *allusion* is a reference; an *illusion* is a false impression. If one wants a word that means m*i*staken *i*dea, one wants *i*llusion.

> ❧ *Miss Kaye told Mr. Brannock that she was under the illusion he would be her Prince Charming; Mr. Brannock did not understand the allusion.*

altar, alter: If one changes something, one alt*e*rs it; one worships before an *altar*.

> ❧ *The pastor will alter the position of the altar so the congregation can see the new carvings.*

among, between: Think division. If only two people are dividing something, use *between*; if more than two people are involved, use *among*. Herewith, a memory device: be*tw*een for *two* and among for a group.

❧ *The money was divided between Sarah and Robert; the land was divided among William, Henry, and Ernestine.*

anxious, eager: These two words are oft confused. If one is *anxious*, one is nervous or concerned; if one is *eager*, one is enthusiastic.

❧ *Mr. Darcy had been anxious about Miss Bennet's response to his proposal, but when she agreed he was eager to begin planning their upcoming nuptials.*

anybody, any body: *Anybody* means *any one person* (and is usually interchangeable with *anyone*). *Any body* refers (pray pardon the graphic reference) to one dead person.

❧ *Anybody can help to search for any body that might not have been found in the wreckage.*

bad, badly: When one is writing about how one feels, use *bad*. However, if one is writing about how one did something or performed or reacted to something, use *badly* (twisted one's ankle *badly*; played *badly* in the game).

❧ *Mr. Henry felt bad about having scored so badly on the test.*

bazaar, bizarre: The first is a marketplace; the second means *strange, weird,* or *peculiar*.

❧ *The most bizarre purchase that came from the church bazaar was an umbrella stand made of crocodile hide.*

bear, bare: A b*ear* can t*ear* off one's *ear*; if one is bar*e*—well, The Author hesitates to express this thought in mixed company, but it must be done—if one is bar*e*, one is nud*e*.

❧ *The bare bathers were disturbed when the grizzly bear arrived. As well they should be.*

besides, beside: If one intends to mean *in addition to*, one must use the word that has an additional *s* (*besides*); *beside* means *by the side of.*

❧ *Besides her bridegroom, the bride wanted her father beside her on her wedding day.*

breath, breathe: One takes a *breath*; if one wishes to breathe, one would engage in the act of inhaling and exhaling.

❧ *In the cold of the arctic winter, it was hard for Captain Smith to breathe when taking a breath outside.*

can, may: If one *can* do something, one is physically able to do it. If one *may* do it, one has permission to do it.

❧ *Mr. Wickham can create a scandal but he may not.*

cannot, am not, is not, are not, and all other "nots": When one is attempting to negate an action by including the word *not* in its description, one writes the phrase as two separate words, with the exception of the word *cannot*, which is written as one word.

❧ *One cannot separate cannot into its constituent parts, but that is not the end of the world.*

capital, capitol: The *capitol* is the building in which a legislative body meets. If one means the building to be found in Washington, D.C., use a capital *C*; if one means the building in one's state, use a lowercase *c*. Remember that the building (the one spelled with an *o*) usually has a dome. Use *capital* with all other meanings.

❧ *The amount of capital spent by the legislators at the capitol is appalling.*

carat, caret, carrot, karat: A *carat* is a weight for a stone (a diamond, for instance); *carat* is also an alternate spelling of *karat*, which is a measurement of how much gold is in an alloy (as in the abbreviation 18k; the *k* is for *karat*). A *caret* is this proofreading mark: ^ (meaning that one should insert something at that point). Finally, a *carrot* is the orange vegetable one's mother boiled to a mush and encouraged one to eat in order to strengthen one's eyesight.

❧ *Set in an eighteen-karat gold band, the five-carat diamond was shaped like a carrot.*

censor, censure: To *censor* is to take out the unacceptable material; to *censure* is to place blame (one must not cen*sure* someone unless one is *sure*).

❧ *The House of Lords voted to censure the MP for trying to censor the novels that his maids enjoyed reading.*

cite, sight, site: One's *sight* is one's vision or a view (one uses one's *sight* to look at a beautiful *sight*); to *cite* is to make reference to a specific source; a *site* is a location, such as the Spanish Steps in Rome.

❧ *A man on the Grand Tour must see the sights of Italy with his own eyes instead of using Baedeker to cite the quality of the sites.*

coarse, course: If something is *coarse*, it is rough; *oars* are *coarse*. A *course* is a route, a class, or part of the idiomatic phrase "of course."

❧ *The course led the horses over coarse terrain.*

complement, compliment: If something completes another thing, it *complements* it (*complete* = *complement*). If one receives praise, one has gotten a *compliment* (*I* like to receive a compl*i*ment).

🔏 *The tiara will complement the outfit the queen will wear, and she will surely receive many compliments on her attire.*

conscious, conscience: If one is in full possession of one's faculties, one is said to be *conscious*. If one is troubled by one's moral failings, one has a *conscience* (it is not a *science* to have a con*science*).

🔏 *Marie said she wasn't conscious of the fact that her conscience told her not to take the shilling from the plate at church.*

continual, continuous: *Continual* actions are intermittent; *continuous* actions go on uninterrupted.

🔏 *The continual rains lasted for ten days; because of that, the Blacksons had a continuous problem with water in their parlor.*

core, corps, corpse: A *core* is a center or main section; a *corps* is a group or organization; a *corpse* is—there is simply no delicate way to put this—a dead body.

🔏 *At the core of Scrooge's sleeplessness was the corps of ghosts that warned him that soon he would be but a corpse.*

council, counsel: A *council* is an official group, a committee; to *counsel* is to give advice (the critic coun*sel*ed the artist to se*ll* her work).

🔏 *The town council decided to counsel the youth group on the proper way to ask for funds.*

desert, dessert: A *desert* is a dry, arid place. The verb that means *to leave* is also *desert*. The food that is *so* sweet is a des*s*ert.

❧ *While lost in the desert, Mr. Templeton craved a dessert of figgy pudding.*

device, devise: A *device* is a machine or tool; to *devise* means *to invent* or *concoct something.* (To dev*ise*, one must be w*ise*. Will one's dev*ice* work on *ice*?)

❧ *The stable hand would like to devise a device that cleans up after the horses.*

discreet, discrete: *Discreet* means *cautious, careful,* or *guarded in conduct.* (Be discr*ee*t about whom one chooses to m*ee*t.) *Discrete* means *separate* or *disconnected.*

❧ *The dancer's discreet movements were discrete from those performed by the rest of the chorus.*

dual, duel: The first means *two* (*dual* purposes); the second is a fight or contest (the lover's jealousy was f*uel* for the d*uel*).

❧ *There were dual reasons for the duel: revenge and money.*

emigrate, immigrate: To *e*migrate is to *e*xit a country; to *i*mmigrate is to come *i*nto a country.

❧ *Ten people were trying to emigrate from the tyranny of their country and immigrate to the United States.*

eminent, imminent: Someone well known is *e*minent; something that might take place *imm*ediately is *imm*inent.

❧ *Charles Spence Bate was looking forward to his imminent meeting with the eminent scientist Charles Darwin.*

ensure, insure: To *ensure* is to *make certain of something; insure* is used only for business purposes (to *insure* one's property).

❧ *To ensure that Lloyd's of London continued to insure his manor, Mr. Darcy remitted payment immediately.*

envelop, envelope: If one were to wrap something, one would be said to envelo*p* it; the paper container that one uses for one's letter is an *envelope.*

❧ *The purpose of the envelope was to envelop the two French postcards that were mailed to Mr. Binghamton.*

everyday, every day: *Everyday* means *routine* or *daily* (*everyday* low cost); *every day* means *every single day* (low prices *every day*). One must use *single* words if one means every *single* day.

❧ *The everyday inexpensive prices of the cattle meant that more buyers came every day to Smithfield Market.*

faze, phase: To *faze* is to *intimidate* or *disturb.* As a noun, a *phase* is *a period of time;* as a verb, it means *to establish gradually.*

❧ *Kitty wasn't fazed by Lydia's announcement that she and Mr. Wickham had reached a new phase in their relationship.*

fewer, less: Use *fewer* to describe plural words; use le*ss* to describe *s*ingular words.

❧ *Their new manor house has fewer servants and less gossip.*

flaunt, flout: If one is so gauche as to *flaunt* something, one shows it off (the way Lady Catherine likes to *flaunt* her new jewelry); to *flout* is to jeer at someone or something in a contemptible way, or to intentionally disobey (*flout* the laws).

❧ *In an attempt to flaunt his new coach-and-four to the girls on the other side of the road, James decided to flout propriety and addressed them directly.*

forego, forgo: If one means something that has gone be*fore*, use *fore*go (a *foregone* conclusion); if one wants the word that means *to do without something*, use *forgo* (the one that is without the *e*).

> ❧ *It is a foregone conclusion that Meg and Marion will forgo sweets when they are dieting.*

foreword, forward: The word that means *the opening information in a book* is *foreword* (it comes be*fore* the first important *word* of the book); for any other meaning, use *forward*.

> ❧ *To gain insight into an author's intent, one should read the foreword before one proceeds forward in the book.*

good, well: *Good* describes a thing; it does not mean in *a high-quality manner*, nor does it mean *correctly*. If one wishes to convey either of those meanings, one must select *well*.

> ❧ *Master Peter did well on the test; his grade should be good.*

heal, heel: *To heal* means *to cure* or *patch up* (to *heal* a wound); among other definitions, *to heel* is *to tilt to one side* or *to follow at one's side*; a well-behaved dog knows how to *heel*.

> ❧ *One might need ointment to heal the blisters one gets from trying to right the sails when the ship heels in the wind.*

hear, here: One uses one's *ear* to h*ear*. *Here* is the opposite of t*here*.

> ❧ *Did Mr. Darcy hear that Miss Bennet is here?*

hopefully: If one means *I hope*, or *it is hoped*, then that is what one should write. *Hopefully* means *confidently* or *with anticipation*.

❧ *"I hope she says yes," said Mr. Darcy as he waited hope-*
fully for the answer to his proposal.

imply, infer: A gentleperson in mixed company refrains
from saying certain things aloud. The unspoken words can
still be communicated, however. A speaker im*p*lies something; a liste*n*er i*n*fers something.

❧ *Captain Smythe thought the commander had implied*
that he would be back for an inspection next week, but
Lieutenant Eggington-Andrews did not infer that.

in, into: *In* means with*in*; *into* means from the outside *to* the
*in*side.

❧ *She went into the library and found the pen she had put*
in the desk drawer.

its, it's: *It's* means only *it is* (before *it's* too late); *its* means
belonging to it (Cook gave the dog *its* food and water).

❧ *It's a shame that the dog lost its bone.*

lay, lie: If one finds the difference between *lay* and *lie* a vexing conundrum, one is not alone. But that does not mean one
must throw one's hands up and use a different word entirely.
Consider: Mary *lay* her head on the pillow; last night she
laid her head on the pillow; in the past she has *laid* her head

on the pillow. One may find it helpful to
remember that the forms of *lay* (meaning *to put or place*) are transitive (they
take an object). Today Mary will *lie* in
the sun; yesterday she *lay* in the sun;
in the past she has *lain* in the sun. The
forms of *lie* (meaning *to rest or recline*)
are intransitive (they take no object).

❧ *As Scrooge lay in bed, he wondered where he had laid his sack of money.*

loose, lose: *Loose* (which rhymes with *noose*) means *not tight*. *Lose* is the opposite of *find*.

❧ *Will one lose one's belt if it is too loose?*

may have, might have, must have, should have, would have, could have versus **may of, might of, must of, should of, would of, could of:** When those individuals of less-than-stellar enunciation speak, they elide these phrases so that they all sound as if they end in *of*, but in fact all of them end in *have*. Their correct forms are *may have*, *might have*, *must have*, *should have*, *would have*, and *could have*. The Author begs one not to forget this.

❧ *Mr. Bennet must have thought Mrs. Bennet would enjoy going to visit Netherfield.*

nauseated, nauseous: *Nauseous* is often misused; it means *disgusting* or *sickening*; *nauseated* means *sick to one's stomach* (one can get nause*ate*d from something one *ate*).

❧ *The nauseous fumes caused the miners to become nauseated.*

pair, pear: The first has to do with two (*pair* of dueling pistols; to *pair* up for the waltz); the second is a fruit (one may *eat* a pear).

❧ *The romantic pair bought a pear to share on their picnic.*

passed, past: *Passed* is a verb; *past* is an adjective (p*ast* often means l*ast*) or noun meaning *the preceding time*.

❧ *In the past, the parson had passed by Lady Catherine's estate on many occasions.*

peak, peek, pique: A *peak* is a *high point,* like a mountain peak (think of the shape of the *A* in PE*A*K); to p*ee*k at something is to try to s*ee* it; to *pique* is to *intrigue* or *stimulate.*

> ❧ *Mr. Barnum tried to pique the children's interest in his carnival by telling them that they could peek through the curtain to see the bearded lady when they reached the midway at the peak of the hill.*

pore, pour: If one attempts to *read something carefully,* one is said to *pore* over it. If one makes a liquid go *out* of a container, one is said to p*our* it.

> ❧ *After she pored over the instructions for serving, Madeline poured the tea without spilling.*

principle, principal: *Principle* means *law* or *belief. Principal* means *major* or *head;* it also means *money that earns interest in a bank.* If one must have a memory device, one may try this: The princi*pal* is the head person in a school; he or she is your *pal* and makes princi*pal* decisions. The Author regrets the necessity for including puerile slang in a book of otherwise weighty import.

> ❧ *To treat all students fairly is the most important principle a principal should believe.*

quiet, quite: *Quiet* is *calm* or *silence; quite* means *to a certain extent.* Many otherwise educated individuals, when writing in haste, transpose the *t* and the *e,* creating an egregious error that could be entirely avoided by attending to one's tasks with the time and attention they deserve.

❧ *Are you quite sure that you were quiet in the library?*

real, really: *Real* means *actual* or *true*; *really* means *in truth* or *in reality*. Even in the direst extremity of need, neither *real* nor *really* should be used in the sense of *very*. The Author shudders to offer an example of this execrable practice, but The Editor insists. Herewith, then, are two examples of what *not* to write: That's a *real* good song the musicians are playing; Mr. Bingley is *really* glad that Mrs. Bingley hired that trio.

The Author is now pleased to present the correct usage of these terms:

❧ *When Captain Sparrow realized he was really lost, the real importance of carrying a compass hit him.*

respectfully, respectively: If one is *full* of respect for someone and wishes to show it, one does it respect*fully*. *Respectively* means *in the order stated*.

❧ *Upon hearing the sad news, Mr. Forthright-Browne respectfully paid his condolences by calling upon Miss Bickenham and Mr. Wallace, respectively.*

set, sit: If one were to plac*e* something, one would s*et* it. If one is in an upr*ight* pos*ition* (as in a chair), one is said to s*it*. In addition, *set* is a transitive verb (it must have an object of the action); *sit* is an intransitive verb (it does not have an object).

❧ *The housekeeper said to the maid, "Please set the table before you sit down."*

sole, soul: *Sole* means *only* or *special*; it can also mean the underside of a foot or a shoe; if one has ever been to

Billingsgate, then one knows it is also the name of a fish. One's *soul* is associated with *one's spiritual or religious side*.

❧ *Helen's sole reason for refusing Dr. Faustus's suit was her certainty that he had sold his soul to the devil.*

stationary, stationery: If one wishes to indicate that something lacks any motion, use *stationary*; if one means the paper upon which one writes a lett*e*r, use station*e*ry.

❧ *Mr. Reeve wrote a letter on his embossed stationery to complain that the train remained stationary long after it was scheduled to depart the North Berwick rail station.*

supposed (to): Often the *–d* is incorrectly omitted from *supposed to* (meaning *expected to* or *designed to*).

❧ *The butler said to the footman, "In this job, you are supposed to be able to help the ladies into the carriage without dropping them in the mud."*

than, then: If one intends to mean *next* or *therefore* or *at that time*, one must use *then*. If one wishes to make a comparison, use th*a*n.

❧ *For a while, the horse Wickham bet on ran more quickly than the others; then she dropped her pace.*

that, which: Use *which* only when one cannot use *that* and retain the sense of the sentence.

❧ *"I do not know which of my suitors to choose!" cried Caroline, which was the kind of problem Mary wished that she had.*

there, their, they're: If one wishes to express the opposite of *here*, use t*here*; if one means they a*re*, one must use they*'re*; if one wishes to indicate that something belongs to *the*m, use *the*ir.

🦃 *There are the sheep who do not know they're going to get their yearly shearing tomorrow.*

to, too, two: If one means something *additional*, one uses *too*, which has an *additional o*; *two* is the *number after one*; *to* means *in the direction of something.*

🦃 *Before Mr. Wickham went to town, did he ask his two neighbors to attend the ball, too?*

troop, troupe: Both are groups of people, but *troupe* refers to actors only.

🦃 *The troupe of actors performed for the troop of soldiers.*

try and, try to: Almost always the mistake comes in writing *try and* when one needs to use *try to*.

🦃 *The milliner said she would try to get the bonnet in Lizzie's size; Lydia said Lizzie should just try and keep looking.*

use to, used to: *Use to* means *employ for the purposes of; used to* (often misspelled without the *–d*) means *formerly* or *in the past.*

🦃 *Mr. Bennet used to ignore the complaints Mrs. Bennet would use to get his attention.*

who, which, that: Use *who* as the pronoun when one is writing about people except when *that* is required (only when *who* cannot be used). Do not use *which*.

🦃 *The sheriff, who gave the orders that the hunter had to obey, said the estate manager had told him to start arresting people for ignoring the poaching laws, which had never been enforced before.*

whose, who's: *Whose* means *belonging to whom; who's* is short for *who is* (the apostrophe means the *i* has been omitted).

> ❧ *"Whose skeins of yarn are these?" Madame Defarge demanded. "And who's going to stop me from using them?"*

your, you're: If one means *belonging to you,* use *your* (this is *our* cat; that is *your* cat); if one means *you are,* use *you're* (remember that the apostrophe means the *a* has been omitted).

> ❧ *If you're going to the West Indies, be sure to pack a mosquito net in your luggage.*

NONEXISTENT WORDS After one has perused this list of words, one may note that certain words and phrases do not appear on it. This is because, simply put, they are not proper words at all. These are the nonstandard usages that one should never (ever) use in one's writing. The Author would not even bring them up, but The Editor insists. Herewith, then, the words and phrases an erudite gentleperson will always avoid using:

ain't	*can't scarcely*	*nowheres*
anyways	*everywheres*	*theirself*
can't hardly	*hisself*	*theirselves*
can't help but	*irregardless*	

CHAPTER ❷
PARTS OF SPEECH

I f one endeavors to speak and write as a gentleperson should—if one wishes to avoid base and ignoble uses—one must first learn the elements of the language, its very building blocks. With this understanding, one can then place the blocks one upon the other and build a majestic cathedral, or at least a passable English sentence.

What are these building blocks? To wit: each and every word in the English language is categorized according to its syntactical function, that is, its use in a given sentence. These are the parts of speech. By understanding them, one can avoid foolish blunders and master the art of using the right word in the right place.

To begin, dear reader, let us look in turn at each of the categories that comprise the parts of speech: nouns, pronouns, adjectives, verbs, adverbs, prepositions, conjunctions, and interjections.

Nouns

A **noun** simply gives the name of a person *(Cecil, man)*, place *(New Amsterdam, city)*, thing *(carriage, horse)*, or idea *(philosophy, love)*.

How clever of one to notice that some of the nouns given above are capitalized while others are not. **Proper nouns** (particular persons, places, things, or ideas) are capitalized, whereas **common nouns** (generic names of persons, places, things, or ideas) are not.

PROPER NOUN	COMMON NOUN
September	month
England	country
Mr. Charcuterie	butcher

Nouns are divided into several other categories.

Concrete nouns name things that can be seen, heard, tasted, touched, or smelled *(daguerreotype, sparrow, water, orchid, brandy).*

Abstract nouns name concepts, beliefs, or qualities *(freedom, imperialism, courage).*

Compound nouns consist of more than one word, but count as only one thing *(Mr. Neville's Titillating Curiosity and Mystery Shop of Frontier Street).*

Count nouns are persons, places, or things that can be counted (and not, as one might assume, nouns that own large properties and call their wives "Countess"). For example, one may have three *hats* or seventy-six *snuffboxes.*

Noncount nouns cannot be counted *(happiness, malaise)* and are always singular.

Collective nouns are sometimes counted as one unit (that is, considered to be singular) and sometimes counted separately (that is, considered to be plural). *Family, clan, herd,* and *pack* are all collective nouns. In American usage, all of these are singular nouns.

Pronouns

By definition, a **pronoun** is "a word that takes the place of a noun." All clear? Very well; allow The Author to further elucidate.

❧ *When Mrs. Annabelle Merriwether came into the parlor, Mrs. Annabelle Merriwether thought to Mrs. Annabelle Merriwether's self, "Pardon Mrs. Annabelle*

Merriwether, but is that actually Colonel Fitzwilliam on the settee? Is the situation just Mrs. Annabelle Merriwether, or is the temperature really quite hot in here?" Mrs. Annabelle Merriwether went to the window and opened the lower part of the window, only to have a number of bees quickly fly right at Mrs. Annabelle Merriwether. Mrs. Annabelle Merriwether said a few choice words, and then Mrs. Annabelle Merriwether began swatting the pesky bees, which had the unfortunate effect of shooing the bees in Colonel Fitzwilliam's direction and causing Colonel Fitzwilliam to be stung quite a few times.

One should immediately note that the use of pronouns would render the foregoing paragraph more comprehensible. Let us, then, proceed to insert pronouns in their appropriate places:

❧ *When Mrs. Annabelle Merriwether came into the parlor, she thought to herself, "Pardon me, but is that actually Colonel Fitzwilliam on the settee? Is it just me, or is the temperature really quite hot in here?" She went to the window and opened the lower part of it, only to have a number of bees quickly fly right at her. She said a few choice words, and then she began swatting the pesky bees, which had the unfortunate effect of shooing the bees in Colonel Fitzwilliam's direction and causing him to be stung quite a few times.*

The Author hopes that this example has demonstrated a compelling case for the use of pronouns.

Types of Pronouns

Pronouns, like jackknives, may be used in different ways (that is, to perform various different functions). One must simply look at the way a pronoun is used in a sentence to determine what type of pronoun it is.

1. **Personal pronouns** represent people or things: *I, me, you, he, him, she, her, it, we, us, they, them.*

🔾 *I came to see you and him today.*

2. **Possessive pronouns** show ownership (possession): *mine, yours, hers, his, theirs, ours.*

🔾 *This book is yours; ours has an inscription from Charles Dickens on the title page.*

3. **Demonstrative pronouns** demonstrate or point out someone or something: *this, that, these, those.*

🔾 *This is his carriage; that is your horse.*

4. **Relative pronouns** relate one part of the sentence to another: *who, whom, which, that, whose.*

🔾 *The chap whom I nearly drove over last night owns this butcher shop.*

(*Whom* relates back to *chap*.)

🔾 *One country that I'd like to visit someday is France.*

(*That* relates to *country*.)

5. **Reflexive pronouns** (sometimes called **intensive** pronouns) reflect back to someone or something else in the sentence: *myself, yourself, himself, herself, itself, ourselves, yourselves, themselves.*

🔾 *You must ask yourself what you would do in such a situation.*

(Yourself relates back to you.)

6. **Interrogative pronouns** interrogate (ask a question): *who, whom, which, whose, what.*

❧ **What on earth is that gentleperson wearing?**

7. **Indefinite pronouns** refer to an unspecified number of things or refer to an unspecified person or thing. Indefinite pronouns include *all, another, any, anybody, anyone, anything, both, each, either, everybody, everyone, everything, few, many, most, much, neither, no one, nobody, none, nothing, one, other, others, several, some, somebody, someone,* and *something.*

Keep in mind that *all, any, more, most, none,* and *some* sometimes are singular and sometimes are plural.

THE MYSTERIOUS CASE OF SUBJECTS AND OBJECTS
The Author is compelled by The Editor to interject a few words regarding the use of **subjects** and **objects** in sentences. Subjects and objects are usually, but not always, nouns. And this is a section on nouns. Ergo, et cetera.

The subject of a sentence can be described as what the sentence is about or who or what is doing the action in a sentence. If one were to say "Mary had a little lamb," the subject of the sentence—who is doing the action—is Mary.

The object of a sentence can be described as what is acted upon. If Mary had a little lamb, then *lamb* is the object of *had*; it is the thing that has been acted upon.

Pronouns are often used as subjects and objects of sentences, but the type of pronoun one uses changes depending on whether said pronoun is used as a subject or object; that is to say that its case changes as its function changes.

"He ran to the dog" is an example of a pronoun (*he*) in the subjective case (that is, as the subject of the sentence). "The dog ran to him" is an example of a pronoun (*him*) in the objective case (that is, as the object of the sentence). A possessive pronoun (*his*) is also said to have a case, the possessive case.

The Author trusts that this explanation satisfies The Editor.

Adjectives

An **adjective** is a word that modifies a noun or pronoun. An adjective is usually a descriptive word that clarifies the nature of the noun—a *red* chair, a *big* house.

❧ *The patterned chaise tipped over under the weight of our guest.*

Patterned gives one information about *chaise*, and *chaise* is a thing (a noun), so *patterned* is an adjective.

Adjectives can be depended upon to answer one of these questions:

- Which one?
- What kind of?
- How many?

One will readily identify that the word *patterned* as used in the foregoing sentence answers the question *which one?* (which chaise? the patterned one) as well as the question *what kind?* (what kind of chaise? the patterned one), so it must be an adjective.

Articles are a special category of adjectives, a category that consists of just three words: *a, an,* and *the. A* and *an* are called indefinite articles because they do not indicate anyone or anything specific *(a house, an honor); the* is called a definite article (it is, indeed, the only definite article in English) because it does name someone or something specific *(the séance, the university)*.

Determiners are another special category of adjectives. These fellows determine to which particular units the nouns are referring (e.g., *the countryside, those ragamuffins, seven pencils*).

One must remember that an adjective is defined by the role it plays in a sentence. It is bootless—the vainest of vain endeavors!—to try to collect a list of words and call them adjectives. This is because a particular word may sometimes be an adjective and sometimes not. For example:

❧ *The tense mood in the parlor became much more relaxed when the little boy arrived.*

❧ *What, pray tell, is the tense of that verb?*

In the first sentence, *tense* describes *situation* (a noun). Therefore, one must conclude that it is functioning as an adjective. In the second sentence, *tense* is a thing, which means that it is functioning as a noun.

Verts

A **verb** is defined as "a word that expresses action or being." It will not surprise any perspicacious reader to learn that verbs that express action are called **action verbs**. Action verbs are the most common verbs. (That is not meant to impugn their character, merely to describe their frequency of use.) One can easily spot an action verb. For example:

❧ *Jane's heart jumped for joy when Mr. Bingley spoke to her.*

(*Jumped* and *spoke* both show action.)

One can group action verbs according to whether they take an object or not. A **transitive** verb is one that takes an object; an **intransitive** verb is one that does not. When one uses a transitive verb, the meaning of the verb or the action is incomplete without an object of the verb. One could not very well say, "I carried to the well." One must specify who or what one carried to the well: a bucket, a cache of gold coins, a song in one's heart.

In other words, to determine whether a verb is transitive or intransitive, one could ask "did to what or to whom?" If there is an answer, the verb is transitive.

❧ *I carried the incriminating weapon to the well.*

Carried whom or what? Since *weapon* (or *incriminating weapon*) answers that question, the verb *carried* is transitive in that sentence.

By contrast, an intransitive verb carries no such object.

❧ *Exhausted after a day at the workhouse, Mary fainted on the floor.*

If one were to ask "Mary *fainted* whom or what?" one would see that there is no answer. There is no object of the verb *faint*, just a subject. Ergo, the verb *faint* is intransitive in that sentence.

A verb may sometimes be transitive and sometimes be intransitive, depending upon how it is used in a sentence.

❧ *The servants always eat after the family does.*

In this instance, the verb *eat* does not take an object. Therefore the verb is intransitive in this sentence.

❧ *The servants always eat bangers-and-mash on Tuesdays.*

In this instance, the verb *eat* does take an object (bangers-and-mash). Therefore the verb is transitive in this sentence.

If one understands the essence—the innermost nature—of transitive and intransitive verbs, then one can more readily make sense of some easily confused verbs, such as *lie* and *lay*, and *sit* and *set*. One will be able to see that *lie* is intransitive (I lie down), whereas *lay* is transitive (I lay the book on the table); *sit* is intransitive (I'll sit here for a while), whereas *set* is transitive (Mary Beth set the vase on the dresser).

"Being" Verbs

Not all verbs are action verbs. Some verbs express the state of being, not of action. Most of these types of verbs are a form of the verb *be*.

Herewith are the forms of *be* (except for *been* and *being*, not a one of them looks like *be*): *am, is, are, was, were, be, being, been.* "Being verbs" also include *has been, should have been, may be,* and *might be.*

❧ *I am a gentleperson.*

(**am** is a present tense form of **be**)

❧ *Yesterday, I was a gentleperson.*

(**was** is a past tense form of **be**)

Linking Verbs

Related to "being verbs" are "linking verbs." These are verbs that equate the subject and the object of a sentence. For example, in the sentence above, "I am a gentleperson" the being verb *am* could be considered to have the same function as an equals sign in mathematical operations.

❧ *I = gentleperson*

The subject and the object are one and the same thing. That is precisely the function of a linking verb as well.

Some individuals, most often schoolboys or those of a naive character, use the unfortunate phrase "copulative verbs" to describe how linking verbs work, although The Author would never use such shockingly impolite terminology.

The list below shows twelve verbs that can often be used as linking verbs.

appear	look	smell
become	prove	sound
feel	remain	stay
grow	seem	taste

How does one determine when these twelve verbs act as action verbs, and when they act as linking verbs? Use this test: If one can substitute a form of *be* (*am, is, was,* and so on) and the sentence still makes sense, then, by jove, the verb is a linking verb. For example:

❧ *The soup tasted too spicy for me.*

Substitute *was* for *tasted* and one has this sentence:

❧ *The soup was too spicy for me.*
❧ *The soup = too spicy for me*

In this instance, *tasted* is used as a linking verb.

❧ *I tasted the spicy soup.*

Substitute *was* or *is* for *tasted* and one produces this sentence:

❧ *I was the spicy soup.*
❧ *I = the spicy soup*

Unless one has been delving too deeply into matters alchemical, this sentence makes little sense, so the verb is not being used as a linking verb but rather as an action verb.

Helping (Auxiliary) Verbs

Another type of verb that may occur in a sentence is a **helping** or **auxiliary verb.** It can join the main verb (becoming the helper of the main verb) to express the tense, mood, and voice of the verb. Common helping verbs are *be, do, have, can, may,* and so on.

❧ *Mary can play the piano quite well.*

❧ *Jonathon has expressed the desire to attend the opera.*

The Principal Parts of Verbs

The phrase "the principal parts of verbs" refers to basic forms that verbs can take. One may have learned these as verb tenses. In English there are four principal parts:

1. The present infinitive, the "to *verb*" form that one sees as the main entry in a dictionary. It indicates action or being that is taking place in the present.
2. The past tense, which is formed by adding a suffix to the verb. It indicates action or being that has taken place in the past.
3. The past participle, also formed by adding a suffix to the verb. It can be used as an adjective to describe a past action: "The cook took the *baked* blackbird pie out of the oven." It can also be used to indicate a situation or state that has gone by ("The cook *has baked* the blackbird pie already"), a repeated pattern that has happened in the past ("The cook *has baked* blackbird pie three times this

week"), and as a verb in a sentence without a subject ("The blackbird pie *was baked* yesterday").

4. The present participle, which is formed by adding an *–ing* suffix to the verb. It indicates a continuing action. Like the past participle, the present participle can be used as an adjective: "The sound of the *running* water disturbed Mr. Blackthorne's concentration." Used as a verb, it looks like this: "The water is running downhill" or "the water has been running downhill ever since the storm started."

The table herein presents the four parts of several common verbs.

PRESENT INFINITIVE	PAST TENSE	PAST PARTICIPLE	PRESENT PARTICIPLE
turn	turned	turned	turning
appertain	appertained	appertained	appertaining
scratch	scratched	scratched	scratching
hammer	hammered	hammered	hammering
bring	brought	brought	bringing
rise	rose	risen	rising
smite	smote	smitten	smiting

An eagle-eyed reader has undoubtedly noted that the first four examples all form their past and past participle by adding *–d* or *–ed* to the present infinitive. Most English verbs do this; they are called **regular verbs**. The last three examples, however, are not formed in the regular way; these are called **irregular verbs**. A cautious writer, one who does not wish to expose oneself to the ridicule of others, will consult a dictionary when in doubt.

Adverbs

An **adverb** is a word that modifies (describes, or gives more information about) a verb, adjective, or other adverb.

> ❧ *Yesterday the quite relieved soldier very quickly ran out of the woods when he saw his captain frantically waving at him.*

The adverbs in that sentence are *yesterday* (modifies the verb *ran*), *quite* (modifies the adjective *relieved*), *very* (modifies the adverb *quickly*), *quickly* (modifies the verb *ran*), and *frantically* (modifies the verb *waving*).

If one is still uncertain about one's ability to spot an adverb when under compulsion to do so, try this method. Ask, does the word under consideration answer one of these questions:

How?
When?
Where?
Why?
Under what circumstances?
How much?
How often?
To what extent?

In the example above, *yesterday* answers the question *when?*; *quite* answers the question *to what extent?*; *very* answers the question *how much?*; *quickly* answers the question *how?*; and *frantically* also answers the question *how?*

Conjunctive Adverbs
Conjunctive adverbs are used to join two sentences into one sentence.

❦ *Mr. Kennilworth owned five hunting dogs. Only two of them were pointers.*

❦ *Mr. Kennilworth owned five hunting dogs; however, only two of them were pointers.*

Some conjunctive adverbs (these words can also have other functions) include:

accordingly	however	nevertheless
also	incidentally	next
besides	indeed	otherwise
consequently	instead	still
finally	likewise	therefore
furthermore	meanwhile	thus
hence	moreover	

One is at liberty to use conjunctive adverbs to join short sentences into more complex thoughts; however, (one did notice the conjunctive adverb there, did one not?) be sure that:

1. One has put a complete thought on either side of the conjunctive adverb.
2. One has inserted a semicolon before the conjunctive adverb and a comma after it.
3. One is joining two closely related thoughts.
4. One has used the correct conjunctive adverb.

A small group of adverbs known as **intensifiers** or **qualifiers** (*very* is the most common intensifier) increase the intensity of the adjectives and other adverbs they modify. Other common intensifiers are *awfully, extremely, kind of, more, most, pretty* (as in *pretty happy*), *quite, rather, really* (as in *really sad*), *somewhat, sort of,* and *too.* However, because one was paying attention to Chapter 1, one remembers that while *really* is, indeed, often used as an intensifier, it should not be.

Comparisons with Adjectives and Adverbs

Sometimes one needs to show how something compares with or measures up to something else. The Author's dear wife, for example, frequently compares him to her former suitors and makes certain conclusions regarding how The Author does or does not measure up.

One may wish to let one's friends know if the gothic novel one has just finished reading is *scarier* than *The Castle of Otranto* or perhaps even the *scariest* novel one has ever read.

In writing comparisons, one can use one of three different forms (called degrees) of adjectives and adverbs:

- The **positive degree** simply makes a statement about a person, place, or thing.

  ❧ *His house is big. Her house is big, too. The Pemberley-Brooks house is also big.*

- The **comparative degree** compares two (but only two and no more than two) people, places, or things.

  ❧ *His house is bigger than her house.*

- The **superlative degree** compares more than two people, places, or things.

  ❧ *The Pemberley-Brooks house is the biggest of all.*

ADJECTIVE FORMS		
POSITIVE	**COMPARATIVE**	**SUPERLATIVE**
blue	bluer	bluest
dirty	dirtier	dirtiest
happy	happier	happiest
tall	taller	tallest

How, then, does one create such comparative adjectives and adverbs? Herewith, the rules:

Rule #1. One-syllable (and many two-syllable) adjectives and adverbs usually form their comparative form by adding *–er* and their superlative form by adding *–est*. (See the examples *tall* and *blue* in the table.)

Rule #2. Adjectives of more than two syllables and adverbs ending in *–ly* usually form comparative forms by using *more* (or *less*) and superlative forms by using *most* (or *least*).

🖋 *Mr. Carstone's rate of expenditure was more unsustainable than Miss Summerson's. Mr. Boyton's rate of expenditure was the most unsustainable of all.*

🖋 *Jane attended dances more frequently than Lydia. Lizzie attended dances the most frequently of all.*

POSITIVE	**COMPARATIVE**	**SUPERLATIVE**
awkwardly	more awkwardly	most awkwardly
comfortable	more comfortable	most comfortable
qualified	less qualified	least qualified

Rule #3. Confusion sometimes takes place in forming comparisons of words of two syllables only. The source of this consternation? Sometimes two-syllable words use the *–er*, *–est* forms, and sometimes they use the *more*, *most* (or *less*, *least*) forms.

POSITIVE	COMPARATIVE	SUPERLATIVE
sleepy	sleepier	sleepiest
tiring	more tiring	most tiring

So how does one know whether to use the *−er, −est* form or the *more, most* form? One must turn to one's dictionary and consult its hallowed pages. If there are no comparative or superlative forms listed in the dictionary, then use the *more, most* form.

As one almost certainly anticipated, there are a few exceptions to the above rules. These exceptions include:

POSITIVE	COMPARATIVE	SUPERLATIVE
bad	worse	worst
far	farther/further	farthest/furthest
good	better	best
well	better	best
ill	worse	worst
little	littler/less/lesser	littlest/least
many	more	most
much	more	most
old (persons)	elder	eldest
old (things)	older	oldest

One common mistake in both writing and speaking is to use the superlative form when the comparative should be used. Remember that if one is comparing two persons, places, or things, one uses only the comparative form (not the superlative). For example:

❧ *Of the queen's two dogs, the Welsh corgi is the friendlier.*

The comparison is between only two *(two dogs)*, so the sentences should be written with the comparative form *(friendlier)* instead of the superlative.

Another mistake, frequently made by children but not to be countenanced in grown adults, is to use both the *−er* and *more* or *−est* and *most* forms with the same noun, as in *the most tallest statue* or *a more happier child*. Remember that one form is the limit. In the examples, *most* and *more* need to be eliminated.

Because some comparisons can be interpreted more than one way, be sure that one includes all the words necessary to give the meaning one intends.

Consider, for example, this sentence:

🔖 *In the horse races at Epsom Downs, Mr. Barstow's two-year-old could beat his rival's entry more often than his wife's.*

When the sentence is constructed that way, it is not clear if the meaning is the following:

🔖 *In the horse races at Epsom Downs, Mr. Barstow's two-year-old could beat his rival's more often than his wife's horse could beat the rival.*

or

🔖 *In the horse races at Epsom Downs, Mr. Barstow's two-year-old could beat his rival's more often than his two-year-old could beat his wife's horse.*

One must always ensure that one's sentences are not open to misinterpretation. Scandal could ensue.

Prepositions

A **preposition** is a word that links a noun or pronoun to some other word in a sentence. Consider, for example, these short sentences:

❧ *Jack and Jill went up the hill.*

(*Up* is a preposition connecting *went* and *hill*.)

❧ *Little Jack Horner sat in a corner.*

(*In* is a preposition connecting *sat* and *corner*.)
Herewith are the most common prepositions:

about	by	outside
above	concerning	over
across	despite	past
after	down	since
against	during	through
along	except	throughout
among	for	to
around	from	toward
at	in	under
before	inside	underneath
behind	into	until
below	like	up
beneath	of	upon
beside	off	with
between	on	within
beyond	onto	without
but	out	

Note that some prepositions (called *compound prepositions*) consist of more than one word: *in spite of, next to, on top of,* and *together with.*

If, even after this explanation, one is befuddled ("but what does a preposition *do*?" one may cry), consider this foolproof memory device. Look at the last eight letters of the word *preposition*; they spell *position*. A preposition sometimes tells the position of something: *in, out, under, over, above,* and so forth.

Conjunctions

A **conjunction** joins words in a sentence; that is, it provides a junction between words; indeed, like a pastor uniting two hands in marriage, a conjunction unites two parts of a sentence. Conjunctions are divided into three categories:

1. **Coordinating conjunctions** include *but, or, yet, so, for, and,* and *nor.* They join words or phrases that are of equal grammatical rank.

   🖎 *Mr. Basil Swinthorpe wished to attend the ball but his sister did not care to accompany him.*

2. **Correlative conjunctions** cannot stand alone; they work in pairs, like pickpockets. They link alternatives or related words. The pairs include *both/and, either/or, neither/nor, not only/also,* and *not only/but also.*

   🖎 *Mr. Basil Swinthorpe not only wished to attend the ball but also wished to dance with Miss Hoopes.*

3. **Subordinating conjunctions** express the relationship between two parts of a sentence.

   🖎 *Mr. Basil Swinthorpe's sister agreed to attend the ball after he bribed her with a shilling.*

The most common subordinating conjunctions are the following:

after	how	than
although	if	that
as in	in order that	though
as if	in that	unless
as long as	inasmuch as	until
as much as	now that	when
as soon as	once	where
assuming that	providing that	whenever
because	since	wherever
before	so long as	whether
even though	so that	while

Interjections

Egad! That, dear reader, is an **interjection:** a word that can express surprise or some other kind of emotion. Interjections often stand alone. If one is part of a sentence, it does not have a grammatical relation to the other words in the sentence; if it is taken out, the meaning of the sentence will be unchanged. For example:

🔻 *Confound it, what's going on?*
🔻 *Blast! I don't know what to say.*
🔻 *What the deuce? Did you step on my toe?*

Confound it, blast, and *what the deuce* are interjections, albeit ones no longer in common use.

When one is expressing a strong emotion or surprise (as in *Stop!* or *Poppycock!*), use an exclamation point. If one is using milder emotion (as in *well,* or *golly*), use a comma.

A note of caution about interjections: a gentleperson uses them in moderation, if at all. In dialogue, interjections are used far more often than in more formal writing (where they are hardly ever used).

CHAPTER ❸
THE WELL-FORMED SENTENCE

By definition, each and every sentence must have the following: (1) a predicate (the fancy name for a verb) and (2) the subject of that predicate. The words in a sentence must contain a complete thought.

What is a complete thought? Ah! That, dear reader, is the very concept this chapter shall elucidate. The Author will consider what makes a sentence complete and how to identify its elements: subjects, direct objects, prepositional phrases, subordinate clauses, and all the rest, including the oft-troublesome aspect of sentences for many writers: convincing the subject and verb to agree.

Subjects and Predicates

The **complete subject** is the person, place, or thing that the sentence is about, along with all the words that modify it (describe it or give more information about it). The **complete predicate** (verb) is what the person, place, or thing is doing, or what condition the person, place, or thing is in.

COMPLETE SUBJECT	COMPLETE PREDICATE (VERB)
The aged, white-haired gentleperson	walked slowly down the hallway.

The **simple subject** of a sentence is the fundamental part of the complete subject—the main noun(s) and pronoun(s) in the complete subject. In this example, the simple subject is *gentleperson*.

The **simple predicate** (verb) of a sentence is the fundamental part of the complete predicate—the verb(s) that are in the complete predicate. In the example, the simple predicate is *walked*.

A sentence may also have compound subjects and predicates.

🖎 *The aged, white-haired gentleperson and the newspaper reporter walked slowly down the hallway.*

(compound subject: *gentleperson* and *reporter*)

🖎 *The aged, white-haired gentleperson walked slowly and deliberately down the hallway and then paused to speak to Mr. Finsley.*

(compound verb: *walked* and *paused*)

If one finds oneself in the quandary of being unable to identify the subject of a sentence, one must simply find the verb and then ask *who* or *what* did the action of the verb. For example:

🖎 *After a rousing game of Blind Man's Bluff, the six youngsters collapsed onto the ground in exhaustion.*

The verb is *collapsed*. If one asks, "Who or what collapsed?" one answers *youngsters*, which is the subject.

One must be ever mindful of the trap of the innocent-seeming preposition. The subject of a sentence is never the object of a preposition, but one will be tempted to find said subject in that location. One must resist this temptation.

🖎 *The leaders of the group planned to meet on Monday.*

One might be tempted to identify *group* as the subject of this sentence, but group is the object of the preposition *of.* The subject of this sentence is *leaders.*

If the sentence in question is a question, the subject sometimes appears after the verb. To find the subject, turn the question around so that it resembles a declarative sentence. For example:

> ❦ *What is Amy going to do with that leftover*
> *bubble-and-squeak?*

One could be forgiven for being uncertain of the subject. To resolve one's uncertainty, simply turn the wording around so that the sentence resembles a statement:

> ❦ *Amy is going to do what with that leftover*
> *bubble-and-squeak.*

Amy answers the *who?* or *what?* question about the verb *is going.*

One must be able to find the subject of a sentence if one wishes to correctly use verbs and pronouns. And one does, or one would not have this volume in one's possession.

Complements

Some sentences are complete with only a subject and a predicate: *She cried.* However, many others need an additional element to complete their meaning. These additional parts of a sentence are called **complements**, and there are five types: direct object, object complement, indirect object, predicate adjective, and predicate nominative. One's eyes have not glazed over yet, have they? One's incomprehension will vanish as surely as the mist on a summer morning if one will consent to follow along a bit further.

Direct Objects

One type of complement that is used with a transitive verb is a **direct object**: the word or words that receive the action of the verb. In Chapter 2, The Author gave a brief discussion of objects. One may refer to that section for further information should one find this section wanting.

Direct objects are nouns (usually) or pronouns (sometimes). One can find the direct object of a sentence by applying this formula:

1. Firstly, find the subject of the sentence.
2. Secondly, find the transitive verb.
3. Thirdly, say the subject and predicate, and then ask *whom?* or *what?* If a word answers either of those questions, it is a direct object.

> *The little girl constantly muddied her pinafore outdoors.*

One must first find the subject (*girl*), then the verb (*muddied*). Finally, one simply asks, *girl muddied whom or what?* The word that answers that question (*pinafore*) is the direct object.

MIXING THINGS UP In order to keep their paragraphs from being too monotonous, good writers often change the word order of their sentences from the normal subject-verb pattern. For example:

> *The soldiers came over the hill, determined to destroy the fortress.*
> *Over the hill came the soldiers, determined to destroy the fortress.*

In both sentences, the subject (*soldiers*) and the verb (*came*) are the same, but the second sentence is written in what is called inverted order—the verb comes before the subject. Be forewarned that the subject must still agree with the verb, no matter the order of sentence composition.

Object Complements

Another kind of complement used with a transitive verb is an **object complement** (sometimes called an objective complement, not to be confused with an objective compliment, such as "Miss Marsh has hair as golden as the sun"); it elaborates on or gives a fuller meaning to a direct object. Object complements can be nouns or adjectives. Consider the following:

❧ *Gerard asked his friend Reverend Burke for a ride back to the countryside.*

In this sentence the direct object is *Reverend Burke* (Gerard asked whom or what? *Reverend Burke*), and the noun *friend* is the object complement (it helps to complete the information about the object *Reverend Burke*). Object complements that act in this way—that is, elaborate on the direct object—are nouns or pronouns.

Object complements can also be adjectives. For example:

❧ *Lydia gave Wickham a dazzling smile.*

The direct object is *smile* (Lydia gave whom or what? *smile*), and the adjective *dazzling* is the object complement (it elaborates on the word *smile*). Object complements that act in this way—that is, they describe the direct object—are adjectives.

Indirect Objects

The third type of complement used with a transitive verb is an **indirect object**. It comes before a direct object and answers the question *to whom?* or *for whom?* after the subject and verb. Here is a formula for finding an indirect object:

1. Firstly, find the subject of the sentence.
2. Secondly, find the transitive verb.

3. Thirdly, say the subject and the predicate, and then ask *to whom?* or *for whom?* If a word answers that question, it is an indirect object.

Consider this example:

❧ *Sylvia reluctantly gave William her last teacake.*

In this sentence, the subject is *Sylvia*, the verb is *gave*, and the direct object (the thing that was given) is *teacake*. To find the indirect object, one would use the formula of asking *to whom?* or *for whom?* after the subject and verb. Hence, one would say *Sylvia gave to whom?* The answer is *William*.

Take heed: With an indirect object, the word *to* or *for* is only implied. If one of those words is actually used, a prepositional phrase is formed, not an indirect object.

❧ *Sylvia reluctantly gave the teacakes to William.*

In this sentence, *to William* is a prepositional phrase, and therefore *William* is not an indirect object. It is the kind of distinction that only a pedant would love, but, alas, there are many such populating the globe in these troubled times.

Subject Complements

Other kinds of complements, called **subject complements,** are used with linking verbs only. (Linking verbs, which The Author described exhaustively in Chapter 2, are all forms of *be* and, in certain situations, *appear, become, feel, grow, look, remain, smell, sound,* and *stay,* among others.) Subject complements complete (give one more information about) the subject. There are two types of subject complements: predicate adjectives and predicate nominatives.

Predicate Adjectives

A **predicate adjective** is an adjective that comes after a linking verb and describes the subject of the sentence. To find a predicate adjective, apply this formula:

1. Firstly, ensure the sentence has a linking verb.
2. Secondly, determine the subject of the sentence.
3. Thirdly, say the subject, say the linking verb, and then ask *what?* If the word that answers the question *what?* is an adjective, then one has a predicate adjective.

Herewith, an example of a predicate adjective:

🖎 *Percival is certainly intelligent.*

Apply the formula for this sentence: (1) If one has stayed awake this long, one knows that *is* is a linking verb; (2) one proceeds to find *Percival* as the subject of the sentence; (3) then, one says *Percival is what?* Since *intelligent* answers that question, and *intelligent* is an adjective (it describes the noun *Percival*), then one knows, or at least deduces, that *intelligent* is a predicate adjective.

Predicate Nominatives

The other type of subject complement is the **predicate nominative** (sometimes called the predicate noun). It also comes after a linking verb and gives one more information about the subject. A predicate nominative must be a noun or pronoun. Here is how one finds a predicate nominative:

1. Firstly, ensure the sentence has a linking verb.
2. Secondly, determine the subject of the sentence.
3. Thirdly, say the subject, say the linking verb, and then ask *who?* If the word that answers the question *who?* is a noun or pronoun, one is in possession of a predicate nominative.

For example:

❧ *That man over there is Jack the Ripper.*

Apply the formula for this sentence: (1) One quickly and easily identifies that *is* is a linking verb; (2) one determines that *man* is the subject of the sentence; (3) one says *man is who?* Since *Jack the Ripper* answers that question, and *Jack the Ripper* is a noun (it names a person), then one can conclude that *Jack the Ripper* is a predicate nominative.

Phrases

A **phrase** is a group of words that acts as a particular part of speech or part of a sentence but doesn't include a subject and its predicate. The most common type of phrase is the prepositional phrase.

A **prepositional phrase** is a group of words that begins with a preposition and ends with a noun or pronoun (the object of the preposition). Herewith, a few examples:

❧ *during the terrible storm*

❧ *after our dinner*

❧ *for me*

In a sentence, prepositional phrases act as adjectives (that is, they describe nouns or pronouns; they also answer the question *which one?* or *what kind of?*) or adverbs (that is, they describe verbs, adjectives, or other adverbs; they also answer the question *when? where? how? why? to what extent?* or *under what condition?*).

❧ *Several members of the parish dined with the parson last night.*

❧ *Adjective phrase:* **of the parish** *modifies or describes the* **noun** members

❧ *Adverb phrase:* **with the parson** *modifies or describes the* **verb** dined

Other types of phrases include:

❧ **Participial phrase:** *Fleeing from the sudden storm, many picnickers sought refuge in the shelter of the trees.*

(*Fleeing* is a present participle describing the noun *picnickers; fleeing from the sudden storm* makes up a participial phrase.)

❧ **Gerund phrase:** *Singing loudly helped the vagabond forget his troubles.*

(*Singing* is a gerund; in this sentence, it acts as the subject. *Singing loudly* makes up a gerund phrase.)

❧ **Infinitive phrase:** *"To go home is my only wish right now," sighed the tired governess after a long day of teaching the children.*

(*To go* is an infinitive; in this sentence, it acts as the subject. *To go home* makes up a infinitive phrase.)

A final type of phrase is an **appositive phrase**. An appositive is a noun (usually) or pronoun (rarely) that gives details or identifies another noun or pronoun. Here is an example:

❧ *My favorite book, a dog-eared copy of* Hamlet, *has accompanied me on many travels.*

Copy is an appositive that refers to *book*. In this sentence, *copy* and the words that go with it make up the appositive phrase: *a dog-eared copy of* Hamlet.

Clauses

Like a phrase, a **clause** is used as a particular part of speech or part of a sentence; however, unlike a phrase, a clause has a subject and its verb.

Independent Clauses

An **independent clause** (sometimes called a main clause) is a group of words that has a verb and its subject and could stand alone as a sentence; that is, the words could make sense if they were by themselves. For example:

> ❧ *The stack of books fell to the floor.*

This is an independent clause. It has a subject (*books*) and a verb (*fell*), and it stands alone as a sentence. Now, look at this sentence:

> ❧ *The books scattered on the floor, and I picked them all up.*

This is made up of two independent clauses. The first—*the books scattered on the floor*—has a subject *books* and a verb *scattered*; it could stand alone as a sentence. The second—*I picked them all up*—has a subject (*I*) and a verb (*picked*); it also could stand alone as a sentence.

Subordinate Clauses

A **subordinate clause** (sometimes called a dependent clause) has a verb and its subject, but it cannot stand alone as a sentence. In order for a subordinate clause to make sense, it must be attached to another part (an independent clause) of the sentence.

For example:

❧ *I had just stacked the books when they fell on the floor and scattered everywhere.*

In this sentence, *when they fell on the floor and scattered everywhere* is a subordinate clause. It has a subject *they* and verbs *fell* and *scattered*. But read the words alone:

❧ *When they fell on the floor and scattered everywhere*

This is not a complete thought, so it is not a complete sentence. Since a subordinate clause cannot stand alone, it is secondary (subordinate) to the main clause of the sentence.

There are three types of subordinate clauses, and each acts in a different way in the sentence.

1. An **adjective clause** is a subordinate clause that acts as an adjective; it modifies or describes a noun or pronoun. It is sometimes called a relative clause because it often begins with a relative pronoun (*who, whose, whom, which,* and *that*).

❧ *That man, whom I went to Eton with, walked right by as if he'd never met me.*

(*Whom I went to Eton with* is an adjective clause describing the word *man.*)

Be warned! Sometimes an adjective clause does not have *that* in it.

❧ *The new novel that I am looking forward to reading is by Jane Austen.*

❧ *The new novel I am looking forward to reading is by Jane Austen.*

2. A **noun clause** is a subordinate clause that acts as a noun; it can be the subject, predicate nominative, appositive, object of a verb, or object of a preposition.

🔊 *Miss Fforde couldn't believe what she heard while on her morning constitutional.*

(*While on her morning constitutional* is a noun clause serving as the direct object of *she heard*.)

3. An **adverb clause** is a subordinate clause that acts as an adverb; it can modify or describe a verb, an adjective, or another adverb. An adverb clause is introduced by a subordinating conjunction, such as *after, although, as (if), because, once, until,* and *while*.

🔊 *Mr. Sylvester came to visit because he needed some company for the evening.*

(*Because he needed some company for the evening* is an adverb clause that modifies the verb *came*.)

Remember to use a comma after an introductory adverb clause, as in this example:

🔊 *Whenever he came to visit, Mr. Sylvester always brought a box of candy for Mother.*

Restrictive and Nonrestrictive Clauses

Clauses are also categorized in another way. A **restrictive clause** (also called an essential or defining clause) is necessary to the basic meaning of the sentence; a **nonrestrictive clause** (also called a nonessential or nondefining clause) can be eliminated from the sentence without changing its basic meaning.

🔊 *The reticule that Miss Bingley was carrying was stolen but Miss Shropshire's was not.*

❧ *The reticule, which was stolen last Saturday, has been found.*

In the first example, the clause *that Miss Bingley was carrying* is necessary to complete the meaning of the sentence. In the second example, including the clause *which was stolen last Saturday* is not necessary in order to understand what the sentence says. In this instance, the clause is merely extra information.

Notice in the preceding examples that *that* is used to introduce restrictive clauses, while *which* is used to introduce nonrestrictive clauses.

Sentence Types

There are four sentence types: simple, compound, complex, and compound-complex. (Rather like the types of headaches one can get upon reading a grammar book.)

1. A **simple sentence** has one independent clause and no subordinate clause:

❧ *The man on the dapple-gray horse confidently rode into town.*

This sentence has one subject (*man*) and one verb (*rode*). A simple sentence may also have compound subjects or verbs, but there may be only one complete thought (one independent or main clause).

2. A **compound sentence** has at least two independent clauses (two main clauses) but no subordinate clause (no dependent clause):

❧ *The man on the dapple-gray horse confidently rode into town, and the townspeople began to fear for their lives.*

This sentence has two independent clauses joined by *and*.

3. A **complex sentence** has one independent clause (main clause) and one or more subordinate clauses (dependent clauses):

❧ *Although he had been warned not to come, the man on the dapple-gray horse confidently rode into town.*

This sentence has one independent clause (*the man on the dapple-gray horse confidently rode into town*) and one subordinate clause (*although he had been warned not to come*).

4. A **compound-complex sentence** has at least two independent clauses (main clauses) and one or more subordinate clauses (dependent clauses):

❧ *Although he had been warned not to come, the man on the dapple-gray horse confidently rode into town, and the townspeople feared for their lives.*

This sentence has one subordinate clause (*although he had been warned not to come*) and two independent clauses (*the man on the dapple-gray horse confidently rode into town* and *the townspeople feared for their lives*).

One can use this helpful information to vary the types of sentences one uses when one takes pen in hand. Variety keeps one's writing from becoming monotonous, choppy, or otherwise tiresome, thereby retaining the interest of one's readers, with the possible result that they will heartily recommend one's book to others, who will then purchase it forthwith, and etc., allowing one to maintain a supply of mustache wax and ink pens sufficient to the cause.

Sentence Functions

Sentences function in four different ways; they can be declarative, interrogative, imperative, and exclamatory.

1. A **declarative sentence** makes a statement:

❧ *Miss Grey does not like beets.*

2. An **interrogative sentence** asks a question:

❧ *Do you think Miss Grey likes beets?*

3. An **imperative sentence** issues a command, makes a request, or gives instructions:

❧ *Eat these beets.*

Nota bene: In imperative sentences the actual subject of the sentence is often an unstated, but understood, *you:*

❧ *(You) eat these beets.*

The Author recognizes that this type of sentence may very well seem rude to the reader. It is offered in the spirit of elucidation, not as a recommendation for how to encourage Miss Grey to sample the beets.

4. An **exclamatory sentence** expresses strong emotion:

❧ *How Miss Grey hates beets!*

Subject-Verb Agreement

The subject of the sentence and its verb must always agree in number and in person. The first part of this rule (*make the verb agree with its subject in number*) seems simple: If one uses a singular subject, one must use a singular verb; if one uses a plural subject, one must use a plural verb. However, one would have no need of this volume if it were as easy as that.

The Perils of Prepositions

A common problem occurs when one incorrectly makes the verb agree with a word that is not the subject. Ergo, one must be certain to find the subject, and one will never find the subject in a prepositional phrase, although many people will look there. One must disregard all prepositional phrases when one seeks to find the subject of a sentence. For example:

❧ *The tray* (has, have) *fallen on the kitchen floor.*

If one follows The Author's clear instruction, one will disregard the prepositional phrase *of drinks*, leaving:

❧ *The tray of drinks* (has, have) *fallen on the kitchen floor.*

Now, one is left with the subject of the sentence (*tray*). Of course, one would say:

❧ *"The tray has fallen on the kitchen floor."*

Finding the Pronouns

Do not allow befuddlement or confusion to arise when a pronoun is the subject of a sentence. A plural pronoun (*both, few, many, others, several, they, you, we*) takes a plural verb. Consider these sentences:

❧ *"Both of them are [not is] coming tonight," whispered Mrs. Worthington.*

❧ *A few of us want [not wants] to go to the fete this weekend.*

❧ *They are happy to enjoy the fruits of their labor.*

Singular pronouns take singular verbs. Some examples of singular pronouns are *another, anybody, anyone, anything, each, either, everybody, everyone, everything, he, much, neither, no one, nobody, nothing, one, other, she, somebody, someone, something.*

❧ *Nobody likes to drink tea that has not been brewed correctly.*

❧ *Much remains to be seen.*

Some pronouns are considered to be singular, even though they indicate a plural number (e.g., *everybody, everyone, everything*). For example:

❧ *Everybody is [not are] here, so we can get started on the séance.*

❧ *No one is [not are] going to complain if you want to host the debutante ball.*

Now comes a tricky rule: Five pronouns (*all, any, most, none,* and *some*) sometimes take a singular verb and sometimes take a plural verb. How does one know which to use? This is the time—the only time—one may break the rule about disregarding the prepositional phrases. For example:

❧ *"Some of the money is [not are] missing!" cried the bank president.*

❧ *"Some of the employees in the bank are [not is] the suspects," replied the magistrate.*

❧ *Most of the tellers are [not is] cleared of any suspicion.*

❧ *Most of the jewelry in the vault is [not are] also missing.*

In each case, one must look at the object of the preposition (*money, employees, tellers, jewelry*) to decide whether to use a singular or plural verb.

Special Agreement Situations

Those are not the only oddities of English grammar. One will encounter many, many more instances, including these:

1. The phrase *the only one of those* uses a singular verb; however, the phrase *one of those* uses a plural verb. Mayhap these examples will help:

❧ *The only one of those people I feel comfortable with is [not are] the prince.*

❧ *The prince is one of those people who always listen [not listens] when I have a problem.*

2. If one has a sentence with *every* or *many a* before a word or group of words, then use a singular verb. For example:

❧ *Many a good husband is [not are] trying to please his wife.*

❧ *Every good wife tries [not try] to help her husband get on in the world.*

3. When the phrase *the number* is part of the subject of a sentence, it takes a singular verb. When the phrase *a number* is part of the subject, it takes a plural verb. For example:

❧ *The number of people who came to the opera is [not are] disappointing.*

❧ *A number of people are [not is] at home waiting for the rain to stop.*

4. When the phrase *more than one* is part of the subject, it takes a singular verb:

❧ *More than one person is [not are] upset about the outcome of the election.*

5. When a collective noun is the subject of a sentence, it sometimes takes a plural verb and sometimes takes a singular one. Collective nouns name groups, such as *cast, fleet,* or *gang*. One must use a singular verb if one means that the individual members of the group act or think together (that is to say, they act as one unit). Use a plural verb if one means that the individual members of the group act or think separately. For example:

❧ *The couple is renewing its endowment to the university.*

(The two people were renewing as a unit.)

❧ *The couple were cleared of the charges of embezzlement.*

(The two were cleared separately.)

6. Subjects that express amounts may confuse some writers as well, as they can sometimes take singular verbs and sometimes plural ones. When the particular measurement or quantity (e.g., of time, money, weight, volume, food, or fractions) is considered as one unit or group, then use a singular verb:

❧ *Four shillings to buy a turkey is [not are] highway robbery!*

❧ *I would estimate that two-thirds of the snow has [not have] melted.*

7. Some nouns look plural but actually name one person, place, or thing, and so they are singular:

❧ *The United States is [not are] extending its trade agreement with the British West Indies.*

(Although there are fifty states in the United States, it is only one country.)

❧ *It is odd that economics is [not are] called "the dismal science."*

(*Economics* looks like a plural word, but it's only one subject.)

8. Here is another special situation: When one uses the words *pants*, *trousers*, *shears*, *spectacles*, *tongs*, and *scissors* alone, one uses a plural verb:

❧ *These pants are [not is] too tight since I returned home from the Grand Tour.*

❧ *Do [not Does] these shears need to be sharpened?*

But! If one were to put the words *a pair of* in front of *pants*, *trousers*, *shears*, *spectacles*, *tongs*, or *scissors*, then one needs a singular verb:

❧ *This pair of pants is [not are] too tight since I returned home from the Grand Tour.*

❧ *Does [not Do] this pair of shears need to be sharpened?*

When in doubt, dear reader, one can always rewrite the sentence.

Using Compound Subjects

The first rule in this part is straightforward. **Compound subjects** (subjects joined by *and*) take a plural verb:

❧ *Mary and Mark are [not is] here.*

❧ *Mr. and Mrs. Claxton are [not is] joining us for an informal dinner tonight.*

There is an exception (not that one expected otherwise): If one has two or more subjects joined by *and*—and the subjects are thought of as one unit—then use a singular verb.

❧ *Cheltenham & Gloucester is where the Smythes have always banked.*

The second rule is *almost* as easy. Singular subjects joined by *or* or *nor* take a singular verb:

❧ *Neither my father nor my brother is [not are] here today.*

❧ *The butcher, the baker, or the candlestick maker is [not are] coming to tomorrow's fair.*

Plural subjects joined by *or* or *nor* take a plural verb:

❧ *The Smiths or the Joneses are [not is] visiting tonight.*

❧ *The horses or the pigs are [not is] making too much noise tonight.*

With the second and third rules, one must be sure that the subjects joined by *or* or *nor* are either *all* singular or *all* plural:

1. If all the subjects are singular, use a singular verb.
2. If all the subjects are plural, use a plural verb.

What, prithee, does one do if one has one singular subject and one plural subject joined by *or* or *nor*? Does one use a singular or plural verb? The answer is exceedingly simple: One makes the verb agree with the subject that is closer to the verb. So one would write:

🖎 *My cat or my three dogs are [not* is, *since* dogs *is plural and is closer to the verb] coming with me on the walk.*

If one inverted the subjects, one would write:

🖎 *My three dogs or my cat is [not* are, *since* cat *is singular and is closer to the verb] coming with me on the walk.*

Here, There, and Everywhere

Sometimes writers and speakers have a hard time with sentences that begin with *here* or *there*. Writing either

🖎 *Here's the money I owe you.*

or

🖎 *There's plenty of time left.*

is fine because if one changed the contractions into the two words each represents, one would have "Here is the money I owe you" and "There is plenty of time left." Correct and admirable, yes?

Sadly, one occasionally encounters sentences such as:

🖎 *Here's the books I told you I'd bring to you.*

🖎 *There's lots of teacakes left, so help yourself.*

In these examples, one actually has "Here is the books I told you I'd bring to you" and "There is lots of teacakes left, so help yourself." Obviously, one would never say either of those, so the verb form is wrong. Since each of those subjects is plural, one needs to use the plural verb (*are*).

So the rule can be written thusly: If one begins a sentence with *here* or *there* and one has a plural subject, one must be sure to use a plural verb (usually the verb *are*).

CHAPTER 4
VERB VARIETIES

One might say that "a rose is a rose is a rose" (or perhaps "a noun is a noun is a noun"), but verbs are not so simple. Even a garden-variety verb, such as *grow*, can go back to the past (*grew*), leap to the future (*will grow*), and change in number (*it grows, they grow*). It can even transform itself into a verbal (such as *growing, grown,* or *to grow*) and do the job of an adjective, adverb, or noun.

Yet do not despair, dear reader! The Author will give one the guidance one needs to master the complexities of all those forms that are tricky or irregular.

Verbals

In addition to the eight main parts of speech, there are three other parts—participles, gerunds, and infinitives—called **verbals**. Verbals are called hybrids because they are part verb; but they do not act as verbs in a sentence, they act like other parts of speech. They give themselves airs, rather like Miss Dunham down the lane.

Participles

A **participle** is part verb and part something else: vague, yet true. It is used as an adjective. (Remember that adjectives answer one of three questions: *which one? what kind of?* or *how many?*) Some participles consist of a verb plus *–ing,* as in these sentences:

❧ *Just let sleeping Schipperkes lie.*

Sleeping consists of the verb *sleep* plus the ending *–ing,* and it acts as an adjective in the sentence. It describes *Schipperkes,* and it answers the question *which ones?*

🖎 *Shivering from the cold, Robert went immediately to the teapot and poured himself a large cup.*

Shivering consists of the verb *shiver* plus the ending *–ing*, and it acts as an adjective in the sentence. It describes *Robert*, and it answers the question *what kind of?* or *which one?*

These are examples of **present participles**.

Other participles, called **past participles**, consist of a verb plus *–d* or *–ed*, as in these sentences:

🖎 *The entire expedition, exhilarated from the unexpected discovery, embraced the local guides.*

Exhilarated consists of the verb *exhilarate* plus the ending *–ed*, and it acts as an adjective in the sentence. It describes *expedition*, and it answers the question *which ones?*

One can easily grasp the principles involved, is that not so? However, on occasion, unmannerly individuals use participles incorrectly and can create a **dangling participle** (also called a hanging participle or an unattached participle). For example:

🖎 *Babbling incoherently, the governess quickly wrapped her arms around the child.*

The way the sentence is written, it seems that the governess was babbling (a participle) incoherently. What the writer means (at least, what one hopes the writer means) is that the child was babbling incoherently. The sentence should be rewritten, perhaps this way:

🖎 *The governess quickly wrapped her arms around the babbling child.*

🖎 *The governess quickly wrapped her arms around the child, who was babbling incoherently.*

Gerunds

Like a present participle, a **gerund** is a word that begins with a verb and ends in *–ing*. Unlike a participle, though, a gerund acts like a noun (that is, it names a person, place, or thing) in a sentence.

❧ *Running up steep bills for the last six months has greatly increased Mr. Alcorn's debt.*

❧ *Captain Gribble thought he could regain his lost honor by challenging his rival to a duel.*

Running is a gerund. It is composed of a verb (*run*), ends in *–ing*, and is used as a noun in the sentence. *Challenging* is another gerund. It is composed of a verb (*challenge*), ends in *–ing*, and is used as a noun in the sentence.

A rule that is often ignored and should not be: use a possessive noun or possessive pronoun (*my, your, his, her, its, our,* and *their*) before a gerund. For example:

❧ *Mr. Forbes continues to be amazed by Miss Blake's [not* **Miss Blake***] singing.*

That is, one must use the possessive *Miss Blake's* before the gerund *singing.* The same is true for this sentence:

❧ *I was upset about our [not* **us***] leaving so early in the morning.*

The possessive pronoun *our* should be used before the gerund *leaving.*

Infinitives

An **infinitive** is composed of *to* plus a verb (e.g., *to go, to carry, to drive*). One will oft-times see infinitives used as nouns, but sometimes they crop up as adjectives or adverbs.

❧ *"I want to go home!" cried the youngster.*

(*To go* is an infinitive acting as a noun.)

❧ *We come to bury Caesar.*

(*To bury* is an infinitive that acts as an adverb; it tells why we came.)

❧ *Mr. Finster was the first man among our classmates to marry.*

(*To marry* is an infinitive that acts as an adjective; it describes *man*.)

Now for the bad news. Sometimes the *to* part of an infinitive is omitted.

❧ *"Please help me finish the dishes before you take the tea out," the cook said to the housemaid.*

Even so, with careful consideration, one can identify the infinitive in this sentence. If one is not capable of careful consideration, or if one is in a hurry and needs a hint, ask oneself, which word in the sentence still makes sense if "to" is added before it? If that is still not sufficient information for one's understanding, one is instructed to turn to the beginning of this volume and commence reading, this time paying somewhat closer attention.

Verb Tenses

English verbs are divided into three main tenses, which relate to time: **present, past,** and **future.** Each main tense is also subdivided into other categories: **simple tense, progressive tense, perfect tense,** and **perfect progressive tense.** These subcategories differentiate when a particular action has been done (or is being done or will be done).

This chart should assist in the elucidation of matters:

VERB TENSES				
	SIMPLE	**PROGRESSIVE**	**PERFECT**	**PERFECT PROGRESSIVE**
	usual or repeated action	*ongoing action*	*completed action*	*ongoing action to be completed at a definite time*
present	hide	am/is/are hiding	have/has hidden	have/has been hiding
past	hid	was/were hiding	had hidden	had been hiding
future	will/shall hide	will be hiding	will have hidden	will have been hiding

Each of these tenses signals the time something is done (or will be done or has been done) relative to when it is being written or spoken about.

The Simple Tense

The *simple present tense* tells an action that is usual or repeated:

❧ *Master William steals an apple from the costermonger.*

The *simple past tense* tells an action that both began and ended in the past:

❧ *Master William stole an apple from the costermonger.*

The *simple future tense* tells an upcoming action that will occur:

❧ *Master William will steal an apple from the costermonger.*

To better understand these three tenses, one might find it helpful to mentally begin the examples with the words *today, yesterday,* or *tomorrow:*

❧ *Today Master William steals an apple from the costermonger.* (simple present tense)

❧ *Yesterday Master William stole an apple from the costermonger.* (simple past tense)

❧ *Tomorrow Master William will steal an apple from the costermonger.* (simple future tense)

The Progressive Tense: One Step Beyond

Use the *present progressive tense* to show an action that is in progress at the time the statement is written:

❧ *Master William is stealing an apple from the costermonger today.*

Present progressive verbs are always formed by using *am, is,* or *are* and adding *–ing* to the verb.

Use the *past progressive tense* to show an action that was going on at some particular time in the past:

❧ *Master William was stealing an apple from the costermonger yesterday.*

Past progressive verbs are always formed by using *was* or *were* and adding *–ing* to the verb.

Use the *future progressive tense* to show an action that's continuous and that will occur in the future:

❧ *Master William will be stealing an apple from the costermonger tomorrow.*

Future progressive verbs are always formed by using *will be* or *shall be* and adding *–ing* to the verb.

The Perfect Tense: From the Past

Use the *present perfect tense* to convey action that happened sometime in the past or that started in the past but is ongoing in the present:

❧ *Master William has stolen an apple from the costermonger every day for a week.*

Present perfect verbs are always formed by using *has* or *have* and the past participle form of the verb.

Use the *past perfect tense* to indicate past action that occurred prior to another past action:

❧ *Master William had stolen an apple from the costermonger every day for a week by the time the constable stopped him.*

Past perfect verbs are always formed by using *had* and the past participle form of the verb.

Use the *future perfect tense* to illustrate future action that will occur before some other action:

❧ *Master William will have stolen an apple from the costermonger every day for a week before his conscience will make him feel guilty.*

Future perfect verbs are always formed by using *will have* and the past participle form of the verb.

The Perfect Progressive Tense: Then, Now, and Maybe Later

Use the *present perfect progressive tense* to illustrate an action repeated over a period of time in the past, continuing in the present, and possibly carrying on in the future:

❧ *For the past week, Master William has been stealing apples from the costermonger.*

Present perfect progressive verbs are always formed by using *has been* or *have been* and the past participle form of the verb.

Use the *past perfect progressive tense* to illustrate a past continuous action that was completed before some other past action:

❧ *Before Master William was stopped, he had been stealing apples from the costermonger for a week.*

Past perfect progressive verbs are always formed by using *had been* and adding *−ing* to the verb.

Use the *future perfect progressive tense* to illustrate a future continuous action that will be completed before some future time:

❧ *By tonight, Master William will have been stealing apples from the costermonger for a week.*

Future perfect progressive verbs are always formed by using *will have been* and adding *−ing* to the verb.

Irregular Verbs

Most English verbs form their past and past participle by adding *−d* or *−ed* to the base form (the form you would find listed first in the dictionary) of the verb. These are called **regular verbs**.

Unfortunately, a number of verb forms are not formed in that way; these are called **irregular verbs**. Here is a list of many of those troublesome verbs.

BASE (INFINITIVE)	SIMPLE PAST	PAST PARTICIPLE
abide	abode/abided	abode/abided
arise	arose	arisen
awake	awoke/awaked	awaked/awoken
be	was, were	been
bear	bore	borne/born
beat	beat	beaten/beat
become	became	become
befall	befell	befallen
begin	began	begun
behold	beheld	beheld
bend	bent	bent
beseech	besought/beseeched	besought/beseeched
beset	beset	beset
bet	bet/betted	bet/betted
bid	bade/bid	bidden/bid
bind	bound	bound
bite	bit	bitten/bit
bleed	bled	bled
blow	blew	blown
break	broke	broken
breed	bred	bred
bring	brought	brought
broadcast	broadcast/broadcasted	broadcast/broadcasted
build	built	built
burn	burned/burnt	burned/burnt
burst	burst	burst
bust	busted	busted
buy	bought	bought
cast	cast	cast
catch	caught	caught
choose	chose	chosen
cling	clung	clung
come	came	come

cost	cost	cost
creep	crept	crept
cut	cut	cut
deal	dealt	dealt
dig	dug	dug
dive	dived/dove	dived
do	did	done
draw	drew	drawn
dream	dreamed/dreamt	dreamed/dreamt
drink	drank	drunk
drive	drove	driven
dwell	dwelt/dwelled	dwelt/dwelled
eat	ate	eaten
fall	fell	fallen
feed	fed	fed
feel	felt	felt
fight	fought	fought
find	found	found
fit	fitted/fit	fit
flee	fled	fled
fling	flung	flung
fly	flew	flown
forsake	forsook	forsaken
freeze	froze	frozen
get	got	gotten/got
gild	gilded/gilt	gilded/gilt
give	gave	given
go	went	gone
grind	ground	ground
grow	grew	grown
hang (to suspend)	hung	hung
has	had	had
have	had	had
hear	heard	heard

hew	hewed	hewn/hewed
hide	hid	hidden/hid
hit	hit	hit
hold	held	held
hurt	hurt	hurt
input	input	input
inset	inset	inset
interbreed	interbred	interbred
keep	kept	kept
kneel	knelt/kneeled	knelt/kneeled
knit	knit/knitted	knit/knitted
know	knew	known
lay	laid	laid
lead	led	led
lean	leaned	leaned
leap	leaped/leapt	leaped/leapt
learn	learned/learnt	learned/learnt
leave	left	left
lend	lent	lent
lie (to rest or recline)	lay	lain
light	lighted/lit	lighted/lit
lose	lost	lost
make	made	made
mean	meant	meant
meet	met	met
mistake	mistook	mistaken
mow	mowed	mowed/mown
outbid	outbid	outbid
outdo	outdid	outdone
outgrow	outgrew	outgrown
outrun	outran	outrun
outsell	outsold	outsold
partake	partook	partaken
pay	paid	paid

plead	pleaded/pled	pleaded/pled
prove	proved/proven	proved/proven
put	put	put
quit	quit/quitted	quit/quitted
read	read	read
rid	rid/ridded	rid/ridded
ride	rode	ridden
ring	rang	rung
rise	rose	risen
run	ran	run
saw (to cut)	sawed	sawed/sawn
say	said	said
see	saw	seen
seek	sought	sought
sell	sold	sold
send	sent	sent
set	set	set
sew	sewed	sewn/sewed
shake	shook	shaken
shave	shaved	shaved/shaven
shear	sheared	sheared/shorn
shed	shed	shed
shine	shone/shined	shone/shined
shoe	shod	shod/shodden
shoot	shot	shot
show	showed	shown/showed
shrink	shrank/shrunk	shrunk/shrunken
shut	shut	shut
sing	sang/sung	sung
sink	sank/sunk	sunk
sit	sat	sat
slay	slew	slain
sleep	slept	slept
slide	slid	slid

sling	slung	slung
slit	slit	slit
smell	smelled/smelt	smelled/smelt
smite	smote	smitten/smote
sow	sowed	sown/sowed
speak	spoke	spoken
speed	sped/speeded	sped/speeded
spell	spelled/spelt	spelled/spelt
spend	spent	spent
spill	spilled/spilt	spilled/spilt
spin	spun	spun
spit	spat/spit	spat/spit
split	split	split
spoil	spoiled/spoilt	spoiled/spoilt
spread	spread	spread
spring	sprang/sprung	sprung
stand	stood	stood
steal	stole	stolen
stick	stuck	stuck
sting	stung	stung
stink	stank/stunk	stunk
strew	strewed	strewn/strewed
stride	strode	stridden
strike	struck	struck/stricken
string	strung	strung
strive	strove	striven/strived
swear	swore	sworn
sweep	swept	swept
swell	swelled	swelled/swollen
swim	swam	swum
swing	swung	swung
take	took	taken
teach	taught	taught
tear	tore	torn

tell	told	told
think	thought	thought
thrive	thrived/throve	thrived/thriven
throw	threw	thrown
tread	trod	trodden/trod
understand	understood	understood
uphold	upheld	upheld
upset	upset	upset
wake	woke/waked	waked/woken
wear	wore	worn
weave	wove	woven
wed	wedded	wed/wedded
weep	wept	wept
wet	wet/wetted	wet/wetted
win	won	won
wind	wound	wound
wring	wrung	wrung

Moods

In addition to tenses, English verbs are divided into moods, which show the writer's attitude toward what he or she is saying. The first two moods, indicative and imperative, are not confusing at all and are used far more frequently than the third mood, the subjunctive.

Almost all verbs are used in the **indicative mood**, which means that the sentence using the verb states a fact or an actuality. All of these sentences are in the indicative mood:

❧ *I'll be seeing you later on today. We'll go to the park with our friends and then have a picnic when we get hungry. The cook will pack a meal in the wicker basket. All of us will enjoy ourselves.*

Verbs used in the **imperative mood** are in sentences that make requests or give a command. For example:

❧ *Please give me the reins.*

❧ *Give them to me—or else!*

The **subjunctive mood** is the one that speakers and writers sometimes have problems with. Fortunately, it is used with only two verbs (*be* and *were*), and it is used in only two kinds of sentences:

1. Statements that are contrary to fact (providing they begin with *if* or *unless*), improbable, or doubtful
2. Statements that express a wish, a request or recommendation, an urgent appeal, or a demand

The following are verb forms used in the subjunctive mood:

PRESENT SUBJUNCTIVE

Singular	Plural
(if) I be	(if) we be
(if) he/she/it be	(if) they be
(if) you be	(if) you be

PAST SUBJUNCTIVE

Singular	Plural
(if) I were	(if) we were
(if) you were	(if) you were
(if) he/she/it were	(if) they were

Here are several examples:

❧ *Mary Alice asked that the mincemeat pies be [not are] served for dinner.*

(expresses a request)

❧ *If I were [not was] a robber baron, I would never have to think about saving money.*

(contrary to fact)

❧ *It's important that everybody be [not is] ready for church at nine, or we will be late.*

(wish or request)

CHAPTER 5
PRONOUN PREDICAMENTS

Though one must readily admit that pronouns are handy and timesaving, one must also concede that they frequently pose problems for both speakers and writers. (Unlike, for example, those cheerful interjections that almost never—thank goodness!—cause any grammatical trouble.) Yet using the proper pronoun is essential to avoid both confusion and miscommunication.

In this chapter, The Author will settle some disagreements, find the right persons, clear up some vague references, solve some puzzling cases, and even discourse upon that age-old "who-whom" problem. By the end, one will be able to use pronouns—even those tricky indefinite ones—confidently and correctly.

Firstly, a quick reminder: pronouns are words that take the place of nouns. They include:

all	hers	neither
another	herself	no one
any	him	nobody
anybody	himself	none
anyone	his	nothing
anything	I	one
both	it	other
each	itself	others
either	little	ours
everybody	many	ourselves
everyone	me	several
everything	mine	she
few	most	some
he	much	somebody
her	myself	someone

that	this	whom
theirs	those	whose
them	us	you
themselves	what	yours
these	which	yourself
they	who	yourselves

Problems with Agreement

Pronouns must agree in number with the words they refer to (also known as their *antecedents*). Read this sentence:

> ❧ *After I saw whom the letters were from, I tossed it in the wastebasket.*

The sentence doesn't make sense because *it* is the wrong pronoun. *Letters* is a plural noun, so the pronoun used to replace it should also be plural. To correct the sentence, *it* must be replaced by the plural pronoun *them*.

Put another way, the rule is this: If a pronoun is plural, its antecedent must be plural; if a pronoun is singular, its antecedent must be singular.

Problems with Indefinite Pronouns

Indefinite pronouns include the following:

all	anything	everyone
another	both	everything
any	each	few
anybody	either	little
anyone	everybody	many

most	none	several
much	nothing	some
neither	one	somebody
no one	other	someone
nobody	others	something

Anybody, anyone, anything, each, either, everybody, everyone, everything, neither, nobody, no one, none, one, somebody, someone, and *something* are all considered to be singular words, so they all require a singular pronoun.

❧ *Everybody is seated, and each is waiting for the coach to depart.*

❧ *Each of the King Charles spaniels needs its personalized collar before it can be enrolled in dog obedience school.*

AN EXCEPTION TO THE RULE Remember the rule that says to disregard any prepositional phrase when one is looking for the subject of a sentence? Take a look at these two sentences:

❧ *All of the money is missing from the vault.*
❧ *All of the teacakes are missing from the tray.*

In both sentences, the subject is *all.* But the first sentence has a singular verb and the second sentence has a plural verb—and both are correct.

With five pronouns (*all, any, most, none,* and *some*), the "disregard the prepositional phrase" rule does not apply. For those five pronouns, look at the object of the preposition to determine which verb to use.

In everyday speech, a common and understandable though nonetheless regrettable tendency is to use *they* or *their* in place of some singular pronouns. In the first example, one might hear the sentence spoken this way:

> ❧ *Everybody is seated, and they are waiting for the coach to depart.*

This usage is called the "singular they" because *they* refers to an antecedent that is singular.

Even though using the "singular they" is becoming more commonplace, its usage is still frowned on in some circles—for example, this one. However, as mightily as grammarians may attempt to prevent it, the rules of grammar do change, and this rule will almost certainly fall beneath the weight of common usage. Using the "singular they" helps prevent an overuse of *his or her* or *he or she*. For example, consider the following paragraph:

> ❧ *When I came downstairs, everybody in the family was already eating his or her breakfast, and everyone was engrossed in reading his or her sections of the newspaper. Each of them seemed to be in his or her own little world.*

Even the most equable among us could find that repetition tiresome, if not mind-numbing, and so a common practice is to use *they* or *their* instead of *he and she* or *his and her*.

> ❧ *When I came downstairs, everybody in the family was already eating their breakfast, and everyone was engrossed in reading their different sections of the newspaper. Each of them seemed to be in their own little world.*

However, this unpleasantness, while less awkward, is still less than ideal. One need not stoop to the practice of using incorrect pronoun-antecedent agreements in order to avoid stultifying repetition. One can merely recast the sentences.

❧ *When I came downstairs, all of my family members were already eating their breakfast. All of them were engrossed in reading their own sections of the newspaper. They seemed to be in their own little worlds.*

One must agree that this is much better.

Vague Pronoun References

As one may recall, pronouns are words that take the place of nouns; antecedents are the nouns that the pronouns refer to. For example:

❧ *Miss Debenham called to say she would be glad to attend the party on Friday.*

In this example, the pronoun *she* clearly refers to a specific noun *Miss Debenham* (its antecedent). But take a look at this sentence:

❧ *Mr. Harrington-Poole invited Mr. Woods to the estate because he enjoyed a rousing game of croquet.*

Tsk, tsk. Just whom does the word *he* in the second part of the sentence refer to—Mr. Harrington-Poole or Mr. Woods? The antecedent of *he* isn't clear.

To make the sentence read clearly, it should be reworded:

❧ *Because Mr. Woods enjoyed croquet, Mr. Harrington-Poole invited him to the estate.*

or

❧ *Mr. Harrington-Poole, who enjoyed croquet, invited Mr. Woods to the estate to play with him.*

Sometimes a pronoun has no reference at all. For example:

❧ *Miss Henrietta Higgins was afraid he would not remember to order the week's groceries.*

Just who is *he?* Unless the man has been identified in an earlier sentence, the reader is left befuddled and bewildered as to his identity.

Remember that an antecedent must refer to a specific person, place, or thing. For example:

❧ *The debutante was elated, but she kept it hidden.*

What did the debutante keep hidden? Was *it* supposed to refer to the fact that she felt elated? In that case, the sentence would read:

❧ *The debutante was elated, but she kept elated hidden.*

That, dear reader, is balderdash and makes not one jot of sense. The word *elated* cannot be the antecedent of *it* because *elated* is not a person, place, or thing. The sentence needs to be reworded something like this:

❧ *The debutante was elated with Mr. Knight's attention, but she kept her feelings hidden.*

Along the same lines, sometimes in a sentence there is a noun that the pronoun refers to, but it is not the correct noun; the correct reference is missing from the sentence. Consider this sentence:

❧ *After a successful fishing trip with his brothers, Stephen let them all go.*

The way the sentence is now worded, Stephen let his brothers go. That is what *them* refers to in the sentence. Unless the only way Stephen can convince his brothers to go fishing with him is to kidnap them, what the writer actually means is that Stephen let all the fish go. The sentence should be rewritten like this:

❧ *After a successful fishing trip with his brothers, Stephen let all of their catch go.*

Here is another example of a pronoun that fails to refer to the correct antecedent:

❧ *The petition regarding the electoral Reform Act of 1832 arrived today. It wants Mrs. Wiltshire's name, age, address, and signature.*

As this sentence stands, the petition wants Mrs. Wiltshire to provide the stated information. But the petition is an inanimate object that cannot want anything. What the writer meant was that the petitioner, the group behind the petition, or someone else the writer had failed to name wants the information. The sentence needs to be reworded to make it clear who *they* are.

❧ *The petition regarding the electoral Reform Act of 1832 arrived today. The petitioners have asked Mrs. Wiltshire to provide her name, age, address, and signature.*

If one does not wish to be mistaken for a raving lunatic or a conspiracy theorist, one must be careful not to use *they* when one refers to unnamed persons; said another way, *they* must refer to people that one specifies. The same holds true for any pronoun, but *they*, *he*, *she*, and *it* are the ones most commonly misused in this way. If one is concerned that one has an unclear reference, one way to test the sentence is to do this:

1. Find the pronoun.
2. Replace the pronoun with its antecedent—the noun it refers to (remember, the noun must be the exact word).

3. If the sentence does not make sense, one must reword one's sentence.

Choosing the Right Person

One may need to write from different points of view, which requires using the appropriate pronoun.

First-person pronouns include *I, me, my, mine, we, our,* and *us,* and the first-person point of view expresses the personal point of view of the speaker or author (*I will bring the book to Jack*).

Second-person pronouns include *you, your,* and *yours,* and material expressed in the second-person point of view directly addresses the listener or reader (*You will bring the book to Jack*).

Third-person pronouns include *he, she, him, her, his, hers, they, them, their,* and *theirs.* In the third-person point of view, material is expressed from the point of view of a detached writer or other characters (*They will bring the book to Jack*).

Shifts in Person

One of the most common problems in writing comes with a shift in person. The writer begins in either first or third person and then—without reason—shifts to second person. Take, for example, this paragraph:

Even in a festive atmosphere I can be embarrassed by someone else, and this causes you to become tense. For instance, somebody you know can embarrass you at a party or during a picnic. It is quite simple for a stranger to embarrass you. This can be upsetting, depending on the kind of person you are; it can be hurtful even if you are mentally strong.

The writer begins in the first person (telling about himself or herself by using the pronoun *I*) and then shifts to second person. The constant use of *you* sounds as if the writer is preaching directly to the reader. That writer does not know the reader and does not know if he or she can easily be embarrassed by others, and so on. Except for the beginning sentence, the entire paragraph should be rewritten and put into first person. Here is one way of doing that:

> ❧ *Even in a festive atmosphere I can be embarrassed by someone else, and this causes me to become tense. For instance, somebody I know can embarrass me at a party or during a picnic. It is quite simple for a stranger to embarrass me. This can be upsetting because of the kind of person I am, and it can be hurtful even if I am mentally strong.*

If one begins in third person (which is the most common way of writing), stay in third person. If one begins in first person (the second most common way of writing), stay in first person. If one begin in second person, well, one knows what to do by now. Consistency is the key.

Using the Second Person

Sometimes one is looking for a more informal tone than third person provides. Something written in second person (using *you* and *your*) will have a more conversational tone than writing in first or third person. For example:

> ❧ *You'll need to watch the mixture carefully, and you may have to stir it quite often. When you get to the last step, make sure you add the final three ingredients slowly. If you add them too quickly, the combination will not blend and you'll have a mess on your hands.*

That paragraph is talking directly to you, dear reader, telling you what to do in your cooking. But look at the same paragraph written in third person:

❧ *The mixture must be watched carefully, and it may have to be stirred quite often. At the last step, it is important that the final three ingredients be added slowly. If they are added too quickly, the combination will not blend and a mess will be created.*

Even The Author, who detests second person on general principles, must admit that the foregoing paragraph reads in a boring and stilted fashion.

Pronoun Cases

Pronouns possess one of three cases: subjective, objective, or possessive. The way a pronoun is used in the sentence determines which case one should use. If a pronoun is used as a subject, the subjective case is used; if a pronoun is used as an object, the objective case is used; and so on.

1. **Subjective pronouns** include *I, you, he, she, it, we,* and *they.*
2. **Objective pronouns** include *me, you, him, her, it, us,* and *them.*

   (Note that *you* and *it* are included on both lists; one will learn why momentarily.)
3. **Possessive pronouns** include *my, your, his, her, its, our,* and *their.* (Possessive pronouns are regarded as adjectives by some grammarians. These pronouns will not be

discussed in this section because writers rarely have a problem with using them correctly.)

Subjective Pronouns

Subjective pronouns are used as the subjects of sentences (whom or what one is talking about). Some examples:

- **I** *am going to leave for my appointment.*
- **She** *is late already.*
- **They** *will never make it on time.*

A problem occasionally arises when subjects are compound. One might read, for instance:

- *His brothers and* him *are going to the races.*
- *Margaret, Elizabeth, and* me *were at the fair for four hours yesterday.*
- Me *and* her *see eye-to-eye on lots of things.*

If these sentences do not make one cringe, they should. The pronouns are used incorrectly in each of these sentences. Because the pronouns are used as subjects of the sentence, they should all be in the subjective case: *I, you, he, she, it, we,* or *they*. Ergo, the sentences should read:

- *His brothers and he are going to the races.*
- *Margaret, Elizabeth, and I were at the fair for four hours yesterday.*
- *She and I see eye-to-eye on lots of things. (It's considered polite to put the other person first, so it's better to word this sentence as written than to write it as:* I and she see eye-to-eye on lots of things.*)*

If one is not sure if one has used the right pronoun, try writing or saying the sentence with only one subject. One would never say (at least The Author *hopes* one would never say):

❧ *Him is going to the races.*

or

❧ *Me was at the fair for four hours yesterday.*

Change the pronouns to those one would normally use when there is just one subject (*he* and *I*).

Objective Pronouns

Objective pronouns are used as the objects in sentences. One would say, for instance:

❧ *Mr. Terence came to see her last night.*
❧ *For the twins' birthday, Mother gave them several new bonnets.*

As with compound subjects, problems arise when there are compound objects. People sometimes write or say sentences like this:

❧ *He gave a smile to Carla and she.*
❧ *Please buy a raffle ticket from Nonnie or I.*

Again, each pronoun is used incorrectly in these sentences. The pronouns are used as objects here and should all be in the objective case: *me, you, him, her, it, us, and them.* So, the sentences should read:

❧ *He gave a smile to Carla and her.*
❧ *Please buy a raffle ticket from Nonnie or me.*

One can use the same trick that one used for the subjective pronoun problem, but substitute the objective form; that is, write or say the sentence with only one object. One would never say:

❧ *He gave a smile to she.*
❧ *Please buy a raffle ticket from I.*

Since the pronoun sounds wrong when it is used by itself, one knows that it is the wrong case and one can swiftly correct it.

Nota bene: Unlike other pronouns on the lists (*I* and *me*, for example), English uses the same form for *you* and *it*, whether they are being used in the subjective or the objective case.

Situations with *Than* and *As*

Another problem with pronouns sometimes arises in a sentence with words that are omitted following *than* or *as*.

For example:

- ❧ *Gregory said to Grace, "I always thought Mother liked you more than me."*
- ❧ *Gregory said to Grace, "I always thought Mother liked you more than I."*

When the words that have been omitted after *than* are restored, the real meaning of the sentences becomes clear:

- ❧ *Gregory said to Grace, "I always thought Mother liked you more than (she liked) me."*
- ❧ *Gregory said to Grace, "I always thought Mother liked you more than I (liked you)."*

(Either way, Gregory seems to be in quite a swivet, does he not?)

The same type of confusion can result when words following *as* have been omitted. For example, someone might say or write something along the lines of:

❧ *My husband finds baccarat as interesting as me.*

This implies that, to the husband, baccarat and his wife are of equal interest:

❧ *My husband finds baccarat as interesting as (he finds) me.*

If that is not what the writer meant, then the sentence must be recast:

❧ *My husband finds baccarat as interesting as I (do).*

This signifies that both spouses are equally interested in baccarat—which, one hopes, is the intended meaning here.

By mentally adding the missing verb at the end of a sentence using *than* or *as* in this way, one will be able to tell which pronoun to use.

Who and Whom

Deciding whether to use *who* or *whom* may be the most difficult of all the problems with pronouns. Does one say, "The man who I called on this morning has gone to London" or "The man whom I called on this morning has gone to London"? How can one decide between "The student who is early will get the best seat" and "The student whom is early will get the best seat"?

There is no need to pull out one's mustache hairs. One must simply try the following method.

1. Firstly, remember to look only at the clause associated with *who* or *whom*. In some sentences, there is only one clause, and that makes finding the right word easy. Often, though, there is more than one clause (an independent clause and one or more dependent clauses).

2. Next, scramble the words of the clause (if necessary) so that the words form a statement, not a question.

3. Now, substitute either *he* or *him* for *who* or *whom*. This will tell one whether to use *who* or *whom*. Use the memory device *he* = *who*, *hi<u>m</u>* = *who<u>m</u>* (the final *m* helps one remember the association).

4. Be wary of predicate nominatives. If a sentence uses a linking verb rather than an action verb, use *he* (*who*) instead of *him* (*whom*).

Try the method on this sentence:

❦ **(Who, Whom)** *came by so late last night?*

In this sentence, no scrambling is necessary. One can substitute *he* and have a perfectly good sentence: *He came by so late last night.* Since one substituted *he* instead of *him* (remember that *he* = *who*), one knows to use *who* in the original question.

Now, try this example:

❦ **(Who, Whom)** *were you writing to so late at night?*

Scramble the words to make a statement: *You were writing to (who, whom) so late at night.* Then substitute *he* or *him*, producing these statements:

❦ *You were writing to he so late at night.*
❦ *You were writing to him so late at night.*

One can immediately see that *You were writing to him so late at night* is the correct formulation. Since *him* is used, one knows to replace it with *whom* in the original question.

The Editor insists that a more fiendish example is required to be certain that the method is grasped. Very well. Consider the quandary this sentence poses:

🖋 *Eugenia worried about (*who, whom*) she would be forced to sit with at the formal dinner.*

This sentence has two clauses, but one should only be concerned with the clause that contains the *who/whom* question. In other words, *Eugenia worried* is not relevant to the problem. Take the words after *about*, scramble them to make a statement, substitute *he* or *him*, and the result is: "She would be forced to sit with him at the formal dinner." Since the pronoun used is *him*, the original sentence would use *whom* (remember the memory device *him* = *whom*):

🖋 *Eugenia worried about whom she would be forced to sit with at the formal dinner.*

Aha! Take that, Dear Editor!

CHAPTER 6
PUNCTUATION AND STYLE

W hen writers fail to adhere to standard rules regarding capitalization and punctuation, confusion and chaos result. For example:

> *when the envelope from jandyce and jandyce arrived mrs barnes opened it and cried out this cannot be she yelled in a voice that was loud enough to wake up the whole neighborhood running up from the coal cellar her husband asked whats so distressing nothings wrong she hastened to reply weve just come into an inheritance from aunt lily now well have enough money to pay our bills*

Obviously, the words are jumbled together without any capitalization or punctuation. If the story is rewritten and uses appropriate capital letters and punctuation marks, then reading it becomes not a tiresome duty but a simple, straightforward process.

> *When the envelope from Jandyce & Jandyce arrived, Mrs. Barnes opened it and cried out. "This cannot be!" she shouted in a voice that was loud enough to wake up the whole neighborhood.*
>
> *Running up from the coal cellar, her husband asked, "What's so distressing?"*
>
> *"Nothing's wrong," she hastened to reply. "We've just come into an inheritance from Aunt Lily. Now we'll have enough money to pay our bills."*

Much better, would one not say so? The same words are used, but now one can easily read and understand the story because capital letters and punctuation marks have been correctly inserted.

Ending a Sentence

The best place to begin is at the end—of sentences, that is. There are three marks that signal that a sentence is over: a period, a question mark, and an exclamation point.

Periods

A **period** is most often used to signal the end of a declarative sentence (one that states a fact) or an imperative sentence (one that gives a command or states a request). For example:

⚐ **Declarative sentence:** *A number of operagoers stopped attending the opera after the venue was changed.*

⚐ **Imperative sentence:** *Hand me the pen that rolled near you.*

Periods are also used in abbreviations: *Dr., Mr., Mrs., Rev., i.e., etc.,* and *et al.*

Question Marks

A **question mark** goes at the end of a direct question. It is also used to show that there is doubt or uncertainty about something written in the sentence, such as a name, a date, or a word. In birth and death dates, such as (?–1565), the question mark means that the date has not been verified.

⚐ *Does Mr. Derby wish to attend the concert?*

(a direct question)

⚐ *The local constable says he overheard a man named Richard-O (?) being talked about in connection with the theft.*

(uncertainty about the person's name)

🖉 *The prince said he would donate five thousand pounds (?) to the charity.*

(uncertainty about the exact amount of the donation)

Be sure to include question marks that are parts of titles:

🖉 *I read an article in the* **Illustrated London News** *called "When Will the Queen Marry?"*

If one has a series of questions that are not complete sentences, a question mark should be included after each fragment:

🖉 *Can you believe that it's ten below zero? or that it's snowing? or that my fire has gone out? or that I don't have any coal left? or that I'm completely out of brandy to get me through this weather?*

Exclamation Points

An **exclamation point** (exclamation mark) is used to express strong feelings. While it is true that gentlepersons are discouraged from having strong feelings, sometimes they cannot be helped and an exclamation mark can be used to express the gentleperson's consternation. There is quite a difference between these two sentences:

🖉 *Out of the blue, Mr. Darcy asked for Miss Bennet's hand in marriage.*
🖉 *Out of the blue, Mr. Darcy asked for Miss Bennet's hand in marriage!*

The second sentence tells the reader that there was something extraordinary about the fact that Mr. Darcy proposed to Miss Bennet.

In formal writing, one simply does not use an exclamation point (unless, of course, one is quoting a source or citing a title with an exclamation point). In informal writing, such as in a letter to one's sister, one might include exclamation points after information that one finds to be remarkable or information that one is excited about:

🖎 *The prince said that he would donate five thousand pounds (!) to the charity.*

or

🖎 *The prince said that he would donate five thousand pounds to the charity!*

As with question marks, one should check to see if an exclamation point is part of a title. If it is, one must be sure to include it:

🖎 *I read an article in the* Illustrated London News *called "The Queen Finally Marries!"*

Quotation Marks

The most common use of **quotation marks** ("/") is to show the reader the exact words a person said, in the exact order the person spoke them. This is called a direct quotation. Note the difference in the following sentences:

🖎 **Direct quotation:** *Mrs. Waddlesworth said, "Please pass the grouse."*

🖎 **Indirect quotation:** *Mrs. Waddlesworth said to pass the grouse.*

The same meaning is conveyed either way, but the use of quotation marks tells the reader that the words are being stated exactly as they were spoken.

One of the most common mistakes made with quotation marks is to use them immediately after a word such as *said* or *asked* in sentences that are actually indirect quotations (that is, not the exact words, in the exact order, that the speaker used). For example:

❧ **Correct:** *Harry asked if Anna would pass him the butter.*
❧ **Incorrect:** *Harry asked, "If Anna would pass him the butter."*

Some Guidelines for Quotations

Guideline #1. Every time the speaker changes, one must indent and make a new paragraph, even if the person quoted is just saying one word. This allows the reader to keep straight who is saying what, a worthy consideration. For example:

❧ *Nick looked out the window and called, "Hello? Who's out there?" A voice asked, "Who is this?" "Nick." "Nick who?" "Well, who is this?" "You know very well who this is."*

Written that way, it is difficult for the reader to follow who is saying what. The dialogue should start a new paragraph each time the speaker changes. That way, the reader can identify the speaker. This is the way the passage should be written:

❧ *Nick looked out the window and called, "Hello? Who's out there?"*
A voice asked, "Who is this?"

"Nick."

"Nick who?"

"Well, who is this?"

"You know very well who this is."

Guideline #2. If one is quoting more than one sentence from the same source (a person or a manuscript), put the closing quotation marks at the end of the speaker's last sentence, not at the end of each sentence. For example:

❧ *At breakfast, Geoff said to the cook, "I'll start with a cup of coffee and a large orange juice. Then I want scrambled eggs, bacon, and toast for breakfast. May I get marmalade with that?"*

Note that there are no quotation marks after *juice* or *breakfast*. That tells the reader that Geoff hasn't finished speaking.

Guideline #3. If one is quoting more than one paragraph from the same source (a person or a manuscript), put beginning quotation marks at the start of each paragraph of the quote and closing quotation marks at the end *only*. This lets the reader know that the words come from the same source, without any interruption. For example:

❧ *The blackmail letter read:*

"We know what you've been doing with the parson after choir practice. If you want us to keep quiet, then you'll give us a little money to forget what we saw.

"Don't try anything foolish. If you do, we'll tell everyone what we saw. You wouldn't want your husband to know, would you? We've heard that Mr. Burke takes a dim view of such matters.

> *"Put the money in an old purse and leave it on the last*
> *pew after tomorrow's choir practice. That will end your*
> *troubles."*

Note that at the end of the first paragraph the word *saw* does not have quotation marks after it, nor does the word *matters* at the end of the second paragraph. There are, however, quotation marks at the beginning and end of the third paragraph. This shows the reader that the same person is speaking or the same source is being quoted. The closing quotation marks designate when the quotation ends.

Guideline #4. Use quotation marks to enclose the titles of short works (short poems, short stories, titles of articles from magazines or newspapers, essays, chapters of books, songs, and so on):

- *Harry read a chapter called "The Art and Architec-*
  ture of Old Houses" in a book titled **Motifs of Gothic**
  Romances.
- *She particularly enjoyed the song "It Shall Not Be,"*
  which is from the opera **Ivanhoe.**

Guideline #5. If one is using slang, technical terms, or other expressions outside the normal usage, one should carefully enclose them in quotation marks:

- *My grandmother didn't know what I meant when I said*
  the thieves ran as soon as they saw the "blue bottle." I
  explained that "blue bottle" means "policeman."
- *What does "flying the blue pigeon" mean?*

Guideline #6. Remember that periods and commas go *inside* closing quotation marks; colons and semicolons go *outside* closing quotation marks. This may not always look right (and it is not adhered to in British English), but that is the way it is done in the United States. Consider this sentence:

> ❧ *I was reading the short story "Scared Out of My Wits," but I fell asleep in spite of myself.*

See the comma after *Wits* and before the closing quotation marks? Now look at this sentence:

> ❧ *I was reading the short story "Scared Out of My Wits"; I didn't find it to be scary at all.*

The semicolon is *outside* the closing quotation marks after *Wits*.

Guideline #7. The two other end marks of punctuation—the question mark and the exclamation mark—go either *inside* or *outside* the closing marks, depending on what is being quoted. A question mark, for instance, goes *inside* the closing quotation if what is being quoted is a question:

> ❧ *Martha said, "Did you fall asleep reading the story?"*

The actual words that Martha said form the question, so the question mark goes *inside* the closing quotation mark. Exclamation marks are used in the same way:

> ❧ *Martha shouted, "I hope you know what you're doing!"*

Now take a look at this example:

> ❧ *Did Martha say, "You must have fallen asleep"?*

The actual words that Martha said ("You must have fallen asleep") do not form a question; the sentence as a whole does. The question mark goes *outside* the closing quotation marks to show the reader that. Look at this example:

> ❧ *Martha actually said, "You must be right"!*

Again, the actual words that Martha said do not form an exclamation; the sentence as a whole does, so the exclamation mark goes *outside* the closing quotation marks.

What does one do when both the sentence as a whole *and* the words being quoted form a question or an exclamation? Despite the temptation to employ a plethora of punctuation, use only *one* end mark (question mark or exclamation mark) and put it *inside* the closing quotation marks. Look at this example:

❧ *Did I hear Martha say, "Who came by this afternoon?"*

Single Quotation Marks

In the United States (as opposed to Merry Olde England), **single quotation marks** are used for a quotation within a quotation:

❧ *"Mr. Snopes said, 'I'll be fine,' but then he collapsed," cried the milliner.*
❧ *"I'm reading the story 'The Opened Crypt and Other Mysteries,'" said the butler.*

What Mr. Snopes said ("I'll be fine") and the name of the short story ("The Opened Crypt and Other Mysteries") would normally be enclosed with double quotation marks. But since these phrases come inside material that already is in double quotation marks, one must let the reader know where the quotation (or title) begins by using a single quotation mark.

Using Apostrophes

People often become confused about the purpose of apostrophes and end up misusing them in amusing but incorrect ways. If one were to walk along a market street, one would see signs similar to the following with incorrect uses of the apostrophe:

> *Special price's this week! Buy two cantaloupe's for the price of one! Five can's for $1.00!*

None of these words needs an apostrophe. Each is a simple plural, and one does not need to use an apostrophe to indicate a plural.

Using an apostrophe need not be difficult. Forthwith, the common uses of the apostrophe.

Contractions

An apostrophe often indicates that at least one letter has been omitted from a word. This is called a contraction. For example, the contraction *don't* stands for *do not*; the *o* in *not* has been omitted and the apostrophe takes its place. *I'll* is a form of *I will*; in this case the *wi* of *will* has been omitted.

Other examples:

FULL FORM	CONTRACTION
is not	isn't
cannot	can't
she will	she'll
you have	you've
he is	he's

Possession

Before using an apostrophe, make sure that a phrase actually denotes possession and is not simply a plural. For instance, in the phrase *the babies' rattles*, the babies possess rattles (so an apostrophe is used); however, in the phrase *the babies in their cribs*, the babies are not possessing anything (they are simply in their cribs) so an apostrophe is not needed.

Mayhap some guidelines would help one to make sense of it all?

Guideline #1. If a singular noun does not end in −*s*, its possessive does end in −*'s*. For example:

☞ *The cats scratching was bothersome to Vivian.*

The word *cats* needs an apostrophe to indicate possession, but where? If it is one cat, then *cat* is singular and doesn't end in −*s*, so the original should be punctuated −*'s*. You should have:

☞ *The cat's scratching was bothersome to Vivian.*

Other examples of singular nouns with apostrophes:

☞ *Charlotte's dress*
☞ *the lion's mane*
☞ *a book's pages*

Guideline #2. When one has plural nouns that end in −*s* (and most plural nouns do), add an apostrophe after the final −*s*. Consider this sentence:

☞ *The girls boots were left in the cloakroom.*

Since there is more than one girl who left her boots in the cloakroom, the apostrophe goes after the final −*s*.

☞ *The girls' boots were left in the cloakroom.*

Other examples of plural nouns with apostrophes:

❧ *five musicians' instruments*
❧ *twenty-four years' worth*
❧ *ten trees' branches*

Although most English plurals end in −*s* or −*es*, there are a number of exceptions, such as *children, women* (not to mention *men*), and *deer*. If a plural does not end in −*s*, the possessive is formed with an −*'s* (that is, one treats it as if it were singular):

❧ *the children's coats*
❧ *the deer's antlers*
❧ *the oxen's yokes*

Guideline #3. If a singular word ends in −*s*, form its possessive by adding −*'s* (except in situations in which pronunciation would then be rendered difficult, such as *Moses* or *Achilles*). Look at this sentence:

❧ *Julie Jones help was invaluable in finding a new dressmaker.*

Since *Jones* is singular and ends in −*s*, one shows its possessive by adding −*'s*. Therefore, the sentence should be punctuated this way:

❧ *Julie Jones's help was invaluable in finding a new dressmaker.*

In some cases, an employer or publisher prefers to leave off the −*s* after the apostrophe:

❧ *Julie Jones' help was invaluable in finding a new dressmaker.*

This is often the situation with common nouns:

❧ *The class' grades were poor.*

instead of

❧ *The class's grades were poor.*

Joint Versus Individual Possession

One can use apostrophes to show joint possession versus individual possession. Consider this sentence:

❧ *Mr. Craft and Mr. Poindexters horses were stolen.*

The question is, did Mr. Craft and Mr. Poindexter own the horses together or separately? If, for example, they were in business together as horse trainers, and they had the misfortune of having two of their horses stolen, then the sentence would be punctuated this way:

❧ *Mr. Craft and Mr. Poindexter's horses were stolen.*

The possessive is used after the last person's name *only*. This usage tells the reader that Mr. Craft and Mr. Poindexter had joint ownership of the horses.

But suppose the two were simply neighbors, and there was a rash of horse thefts in Derbyshire. The sentence would then be punctuated this way:

❧ *Mr. Craft's and Mr. Poindexter's horses were stolen.*

The possessive is used after *both* names. This usage tells the reader that Mr. Craft and Mr. Poindexter had separate ownership of the horses.

Commas

When readers see a **comma**, they know that there is a slight pause, and they can tell how particular words or phrases relate to other parts of the sentence. Consider this sentence:

❧ *Will you call on Mary Alice Lee and Jason or should I?*

Depending on where one puts commas in this sentence, its meaning is changed.

❧ *Will you call on Mary, Alice, Lee, and Jason, or should I?*
❧ *Will you call on Mary Alice, Lee, and Jason, or should I?*
❧ *Will you call on Mary, Alice Lee, and Jason, or should I?*

Commas with a Series

If one has a series of items, use a comma to separate the items. For example:

❧ *The filly a two-year-old and Mr. Davenport's stallion were sold at auction.*

How many horses were involved? With the following punctuation, one would see that three horses were involved:

❧ *The filly, a two-year-old, and Mr. Davenport's stallion were sold at auction.*

However, a slightly different punctuation would show that only two horses were involved:

❧ *The filly (a two-year-old) and Mr. Davenport's stallion were sold at auction.*

or

❧ *The filly—a two-year-old—and Mr. Davenport's stallion were sold at auction.*

Use a comma between two or more adjectives that modify a noun:

❧ *The man in the torn, tattered jacket moved quickly through the crowded, dark street.*

If the first adjective modifies the idea expressed by the combination of subsequent adjectives and the noun, then one does not need commas. For example:

❧ *Many countries do not have stable central governments.*

Since *central governments* would be considered a single unit, it is not necessary to separate it from the adjective modifying it *(stable)* with a comma.

If one is using *and, or,* or *nor* to connect the items in the series, one does not use commas:

❧ *The flag is red and white and blue.*
❧ *The flag might be red or white or blue.*
❧ *The flag is neither red nor white nor blue.*

Commas with Compound Sentences

If one has two independent clauses (that is, two complete thoughts that could stand alone as sentences) and they are joined by the coordinating conjunctions *but, or, yet, so, for, and,* or *not,* join them with a comma:

❧ *It was more than three hours past dinnertime, and everybody was grumbling about being hungry.*

The exception: One may eliminate the comma if the two independent clauses are short and if there would be no danger of confusion were the comma not in the sentence. For example:

❧ *We visited the Tate and we went on our way.*

If one has a simple sentence with a compound verb, one does not put a comma between the verbs:

❧ *I wanted to get some rest [no comma] but needed to get more work done.*

Commas with Quoted Material

If a quoted sentence is interrupted by words such as *he said* or *she replied*, use commas in this way:

❧ *"For this contest," he said, "you need three pencils and two pieces of paper."*

Note that the first comma goes before the closing quotation mark and the second comma goes before the beginning quotation mark.

If the words being quoted make up a question or an exclamation, do not include a comma:

❧ *"Put that down right now!" the shoemaker cried.*

Commas with Clauses, Phrases, Appositives, and Introductory Words

Use commas to set apart clauses (groups of words that have a subject and a predicate), participle phrases, and appositives (words or phrases that give information about a noun or pronoun) that are not necessary to the meaning of the sentence.

Consider this sentence:

❧ *The handsome man over there, the only one who works in the haberdashery department of Harrods, has black hair and brown eyes.*

If one took out the clause *the only one who works in the haberdashery department of Harrods*, one would still have the same essential parts of the sentence. One does not need to know where the man works in order to learn his hair and eye color.

If one is not sure, take out the part of the sentence in question and read the sentence without it. If the sentence makes sense, then the part should have commas around it.

❧ *The handsome man over there has black hair and brown eyes.*

Now consider:

❧ *The only man who works in the haberdashery department of Harrods was arrested for stealing four spools of thread and five silk ribbons.*

In this case, if one removed *who works in the haberdashery department of Harrods*, one would have *The only man was arrested for stealing four spools of thread and five silk ribbons.* That is not at all the meaning of the original sentence. *Remember:* If one needs the extra words for the meaning, one does not need the commas.

Commas are also needed after introductory words such as exclamations, common expressions, and names used in direct address that are not necessary for the meaning of a sentence. If one has words that begin a sentence and one could understand the sentence without them, use a comma to separate them from the rest of the sentence. For example:

❧ *My, don't you look nice tonight!*
❧ *Catherine, please help your brother find his tin soldiers.*
❧ *If you must know, I have been pining for Captain Burrows for the past ten years.*

A comma is also used before these same types of words and phrases when they appear at the end of a sentence, as long as they are not necessary for the meaning:

❧ *Didn't you enjoy* **The Mysteries of Udolpho,** *Jean Marie?*
❧ *You'll be coming with us to church on Sunday, I should hope.*

Use commas around words that interrupt a sentence (called **parenthetical expressions**), as long as the words are not necessary for the meaning:

🔖 *The answer to the next question, Miss Pendleton, can be found on page thirty-six.*

🔖 *This book, unlike the one I read before, is written in French.*

Use a comma after an introductory verbal (remember that a verbal is a participle, gerund, or infinitive) or verbal phrase:

🔖 *Weeping at the sight of the grave, Mrs. Carstone was nearly overcome with grief.*

🔖 *To try to regain his composure, he took several deep breaths.*

Use a comma after an introductory adverb clause. (Remember that an adverb clause is a group of words that has a subject and a verb, and describes a verb, adjective, or other adverb.) For example:

🔖 *Because the cook forgot to go to market, she did not have enough turnips to go around.*

🔖 *If Glenn comes into town tonight, the whole family is going to get together for a game of charades.*

Other Uses for Commas

1. Put a comma after the day of the week, the day of the month, and the year (if the sentence continues):

🔖 *I'll be seeing you on Friday, February 23, 1852, at half past seven.*

If one is writing only the day and month or the month and year, no comma is necessary:

❧ *I'll see you on February 23.*
❧ *I'll see you in February 1852.*

2. Put a comma after the greeting (salutation) of all friendly letters and the closing of all letters (for unfriendly letters, see the colon):

❧ *Dear Aunt Agatha,*
❧ *Sincerely,*

3. If a person's title or degree follows his or her name, put commas around it:

❧ *Please call on Robert Householder, PhD, at your convenience.*
❧ *The deposition was given by Edward Butterworth, MD.*

4. Use commas to divide numbers of 1,000 or more to make them easier to read:

❧ *Is it my imagination, or are there 1,376,993 rules for commas?*

5. Use commas in addresses that are written out—one after the addressee's name, one after the street address, and one after the city:

❧ *Mr. Harold Skimpole, 1343 Main St., Albany, New York 10010*

6. Put commas after the name of a city and country when used in a sentence:

❧ *Miss Bellingham visited Paris, France, on her way home from Zurich.*

Colons

A **colon** is used to introduce particular information. One of the most common uses of a colon is to signal to the reader that a list will follow:

❧ *For our picnic, please pack the following items: a tablecloth, a parasol, a bottle of chilled champagne, cold poached chicken, and the trifle left over from last night.*

A colon is also used to explain or give more information about what has come before it in the sentence:

❧ *There are a number of complaints that she has against the tenant of Thornfield Manor: He tore the plaster in the living room, his ward stained the carpet in her bedroom, he kept a mad woman in the attic, and he eventually burned the place down.*

In formal papers, a colon usually precedes a lengthy quotation:

In his Gettysburg Address, Abraham Lincoln stated:

❧ *Four score and seven years ago, our forefathers brought forth on this continent a new nation, conceived in liberty and dedicated to the proposition that all men are created equal.*

There are other times when a colon is used:

• In the greeting of a business letter

❧ **To Whom It May Concern:**

• Between the hour and minutes in time

❧ **a meeting at 4:15 p.m.**

- In dividing a title from its subtitle

❧ *My Favorite Punctuation Marks: Why I Love Colons*

- In naming a chapter and verse of the Bible

❧ **Genesis 2:10**

- In naming the volume and number of a magazine

❧ **Punch 41:14**

- In naming the volume and page number of a magazine

❧ *Arthur's Lady's Home Magazine* **166:31**

- Between the city and the publisher in a bibliographical entry

❧ **London: Covent Garden Press**

Semicolons

A **semicolon** signals a pause greater than one indicated by a comma but less than one indicated by a period. The most common use for a semicolon is joining two complete thoughts (independent clauses) into one sentence.

Consider the following sentences:

❧ *The bank teller determined the bill was counterfeit. There was no serial number on it.*

Each of these sentences stands alone, but they could be joined by using a semicolon:

❧ *The bank teller determined the bill was counterfeit; there was no serial number on it.*

Often semicolons are used with conjunctive adverbs and other transitional words or phrases, such as *on the other hand* or *therefore*. In this case, be sure that one puts the semicolon at the point where the two thoughts are separated. For example:

❧ **Right:** *There is more to this case than meets the eye; however, one will have to wait to read about it in the newspapers.*

❧ **Wrong:** *There is more to this case than meets the eye, one will; however, have to read about it in the newspapers.*

Now, as one undoubtedly remembers, there are exceptions to every rule, and the semicolon is no exception to that exception. That is to say, there are times when a semicolon is used when a comma would seem to be the correct punctuation mark. Consider this sentence:

❧ *The manhunt took place in Minneapolis, Nashville, Indiana, Stratford, Connecticut, Winnenan, Oklahoma, Dallas, and Olympia.*

Notice that there are commas after the name of each city and each state. However, the reader will probably be confused about the true meaning of the sentence. Consider that a semicolon is a "notch above" a comma. By substituting a semicolon in places where one would ordinarily use a comma, one makes things clearer by showing which cities go with which states. Look at how the sentence should be punctuated:

❧ *The manhunt took place in Minneapolis; Nashville, Indiana; Stratford, Connecticut; Winnenan, Oklahoma; Dallas; and Olympia.*

Reading the sentence this way, the reader can tell that the manhunt took place in Nashville, Indiana, as opposed to Nashville, Tennessee. Also, the reader can identify that Winnenan is located in Oklahoma.

WHEN SEMICOLONS WILL NOT WORK Semicolons will not work if the two thoughts are not on the same playing field (that is, if they are not logically connected). Look at these two sentences:

🔖 *The teller wore a blue suit. The police were called immediately.*

Although both are sentences, there is no link between them. If a semicolon were used between these two sentences, readers would be scratching their heads, thinking they were missing something.

Semicolons also fail to work if one of the thoughts is not a complete sentence. Consider this example:

🔖 *The police were called immediately; screeching through the streets.*

The first part of the sentence is a complete thought (*the police were called immediately*), but the second part is not (*screeching through the streets*).

Hyphens

A **hyphen** is a short horizontal line; a dash is longer. But the differences between these two punctuation marks go much deeper than just a fraction of an inch.

The most common use of the hyphen is to divide words at the end of lines. The important rule to remember is to divide words only between syllables. Read the following lines:

❦ *Sarah was unhappy with her oldest child, he-*
r nineteen-year-old daughter Miranda. Miranda w-
as still relying on her mother to get her up i-
n the mornings and to see that her various ge-
ntleman callers were entertained while she primped
over her toilette.

See how difficult this is to read? That is because one learns to read in syllables. When the words are not divided correctly, one has to go back to the previous line and put the syllables together. The text should read:

❦ *Sarah was unhappy with her oldest child, her*
nineteen-year-old daughter Miranda. Miranda
was still relying on her mother to get her up in
the mornings and to see that her various gentle-
men callers were entertained while she primped
over her toilette.

If one is not sure of where the syllables occur, one must simply consult a dictionary, wherein the answer will be found. One-syllable words should not be divided.

No matter where the words are divided, be careful to leave more than one letter at the end of a line (and more than two at the beginning of a line). One should not write:

❦ *Beth wondered if the earl would call on her a-*
gain.

or

❦ *Beth shocked the neighbors when she call-*
ed on the earl without invitation.

One should also avoid hyphenating acronyms (such as GBE or HRH), numerals (such as 1,200 or 692), and contractions (such as *haven't, didn't, couldn't*). Keep in mind that some style guides may say that proper nouns (those that are capitalized) should not be hyphenated. Words or phrases that already contain hyphens should not be hyphenated at a line break when possible.

Hyphens with Numbers

Use a hyphen (not a dash) between two dates and between page numbers:

❧ *The Victorian Era (1837–1901) came about as a result of Queen Victoria's rise to the throne.*

❧ *See the section on the Edwardian period (pp. 31–35) for more information.*

Technically, both of these instances use what is called an "en dash," which is longer than a hyphen and shorter than a normal dash, which is usually called an "em dash."

Another common use of the hyphen comes when numbers are written as words instead of numerals. The rule is to hyphenate numbers from twenty-one to ninety-nine.

Hyphens with Compound Adjectives

When a compound adjective (two or more adjectives that go together to form one thought or image) precedes the noun it modifies, it should be hyphenated. Look at these sentences:

❧ *Charles Dickens was a nineteenth-century writer.*

In this case, *nineteenth-century* is used as an adjective (it modifies the noun *writer*), and so it is hyphenated. Notice the difference:

❧ *Charles Dickens was a writer who lived in the nineteenth century.*

Here, *nineteenth century* is a noun, and so it is not hyphenated.

❧ *Some well-known scientists are studying the principles of evolution.*

In this example, *well-known* is used as an adjective before the noun *scientists*, and so it is hyphenated.

❧ *Some scientists studying the principles of evolution are well known.*

Since *well known* follows the noun here, it is not hyphenated.

Another situation in which one does not hyphenate a compound modifier—even if it comes before the noun—is where the first modifier is the word *very* or an adverb that ends in *−ly*. One should write:

a very condescending attitude

a strictly guarded secret

a very little amount of money

the highly publicized meeting

Use a hyphen to join adjectives only if together they form the same image. If they are separate words describing a noun (as *big, bulky package*), then do not use a hyphen. Consider this example:

❧ *The young lady was always surrounded by handsome but loud-mouthed gentlemen.*

Loud and *mouthed* go together to form the image that describes the gentlemen, so the words are hyphenated. That is to say the gentlemen are not *loud* and also *mouthed* but *loud-mouthed*.

Hyphens for Clarification

Sometimes hyphens are needed to clarify the meaning of a word or sentence. For instance, *resign* means one thing, whereas *re-sign* means another. Other words with this idiosyncrasy include *recreation* and *recollect*.

By the same token *a light, blue frock* is different from *a light-blue frock*.

Dashes

A **dash** provides a window for some informality in writing, allowing the writer to introduce a sudden change in thought or tone. Consider this sentence:

> ❧ *Let's just go into the kitchen and—dash it all! I stubbed my toe.*

The dash tells the reader that a sudden idea has interrupted the speaker's original thought.

A dash may also be used to give emphasis to something that has come before:

> ❧ *Theodore began plotting a way to win over the young girl—the young girl who would someday become his wife.*

Another time a dash may be used is when defining or giving more information about something in the sentence. Read this sentence:

> ❧ *Margaret knew that when she finally arrived home, she would be warmly greeted by her sisters—Lillian, Beatrice, Abigail, and Elizabeth.*

The last example could also be punctuated by using parentheses or a colon in place of the dash, as in these sentences:

🔏 *Margaret knew that when she finally arrived home, she would be warmly greeted by her sisters (Lillian, Beatrice, Abigail, and Elizabeth).*

🔏 *Margaret knew that when she finally arrived home, she would be warmly greeted by her sisters: Lillian, Beatrice, Abigail, and Elizabeth.*

Punctuating the sentence with colons is stuffier than using a dash or parentheses, and thus The Author heartily approves. Generally speaking, the colon is reserved for formal writing.

Parentheses

Using **parentheses** tells the reader that one is giving extra information, something that is not necessary to the meaning of the sentence but is helpful in understanding what is being read. For example:

🔏 *For a complete history of Abernathy's association with the occult, consult Chapter 8 (pages 85–96).*

Keep in mind that if the information is necessary for the sentence to be read correctly, one should not use parentheses. For instance, if one is comparing statistics about two floods that occurred in different years, one might have a sentence like this:

🔏 *The high-water mark of the 1899 flood came in early April, as compared to the high-water mark of the 1856 flood, which occurred in late May.*

One cannot put *of the 1899 flood* or *of the 1856 flood* in parentheses because one needs that information for the sentence. However, if one has a sentence written like this:

> ❧ *My latest (and, dare I hope, my last) adventure with my brother's unruly children was this past weekend; I have not yet recovered.*

it is possible to omit the material inside the parentheses and still have the essence of the sentence.

Another common use of parentheses is in giving dates, especially birth and death dates.

> ❧ *Jane Austen (1775–1817) wrote six popular novels.*

In addition, parentheses are used to enclose numbers or letters that name items in a series. Sometimes both the opening and closing parentheses are used, and sometimes just the closing parenthesis is used:

> ❧ *Before beginning to play croquet, one should (a) set the wickets; (b) provide each player with a mallet; (c) check the balls for damage.*

or

> ❧ *Before beginning to play croquet, one should a) set the wickets; b) provide each player with a mallet; c) check the balls for damage.*

Whether one uses both parentheses or just one, one must be consistent when one is naming items in a series. Also, be aware that if one uses one parenthesis only, a reader may misread the letter as part of the preceding word.

Parentheses are also used to give a legislator's party affiliation and home state (in the case of national politics) or city or county (in the case of state politics):

❧ *Senator John C. Calhoun (D-SC) often changed his position on issues, unlike Tennessee state representative G. W. Higgins (D-Lincoln).*

Another—though less common—use for parentheses is to show the reader that an alternate ending for a word may be read. Consider this sentence:

❧ *Please bring your child(ren) to the church picnic.*

Keep in mind that parentheses would not be used this way in more formal writing; the sentence would be reworded to include both *child* and *children*.

Square Brackets

One place where one will see **square brackets** is in dictionaries, where they are used to show the history of the word being defined.

Another use is in making certain that quoted material is clear or understandable for the reader. Suppose one is quoting a sentence that contains a pronoun without its antecedent, as in this example:

❧ *"He burst onto the party scene and began to take society by storm."*

Just who is *he?* Unless the previous sentence identified him, one's readers would not know. In that case, one would use square brackets this way:

❧ *"He [John Passmore Edwards] burst onto the party scene and began to take society by storm."*

Here is another example:

❧ *"It came as a big surprise to everyone at the party."*

The reader would have no idea what *it* was. An unexpected marriage proposal? A lavishly decorated birthday cake?

To explain the pronoun so that the reader understands the material more clearly, one might use brackets in this way:

❧ *"It [the presence of a thief in their midst] came as a big surprise to everyone at the party."*

Along the same lines, one uses brackets to alter the capitalization of something one is quoting so that it fits in one's sentence or paragraph. For example:

❧ *"[T]he river's crest has risen sufficiently to warrant a panic."*

Use brackets for quoted material only if their use does not change the meaning of what is being quoted.

If one needs to give information that one would normally put in parentheses, but that information is *already* in parentheses, use brackets instead. For example:

❧ **The man who established the Metropolitan Police Force (Sir Henry Peel [1788–1850]) did so in the face of an appalling wave of crime in London.**

Normally, one would put a person's birth and death dates in parentheses, but since those dates would be placed in material that is already in parentheses, one uses brackets instead.

Depending on the type of writing that one is doing, one might need to add the Latin word *sic* to the information that one is quoting. *Sic* translates as "thus," or "so," or "in this manner"; it is used to show that what one is quoting has a mistake that one is copying; it reassures the reader that one is not at fault for the mistake. Consider this sentence:

❧ *"This painting was donated to the museum on September 31* [sic]*."*

However, dear reader, we know that "thirty days hath September"—not thirty-one, as above. By using [*sic*], one tells the reader that one copied the mistake as it was written in the original form. Note that *sic* is enclosed in brackets (and many style guides dictate that it be italicized as well).

One may also use brackets to let the reader know that one has added italics to quoted material.

❧ **"The time of the accident is *equally important* as the date [italics added]."**

In some instances, one may use parentheses instead:

❧ **"The time of the accident is *equally important* as the date (italics added)."**

One must be consistent and use either the brackets or the parenthesis and never a mixture of the two.

Italics and Underlining

There was a time, dear reader, when a writer could not easily use italics to indicate stress on a certain word or phrase or to identify a book's title. In those days of yore, with only a pen or perhaps a typewriter, the writer was forced to resort to underlining. Now, however, it is quite simple to italicize words and one generally does not need to underline at all. However, if one is writing by hand, one can use underlining exactly as one would use italics.

The most common use of italicizing or underlining is in titles, but only titles of long works, such as books. For titles of short works—such as short stories, short poems, and essays—quotation marks are used. For example:

❧ *The Complete Sherlock Holmes* or <u>The Complete Sherlock Holmes</u>

(title of a book)

❧ **"The Speckled Band"**

(title of a short story)

Note that the titles of sacred books do not require any special formatting or punctuation, nor do books of the Bible.

❧ **I read the Bible for a half an hour today.**

❧ **A copy of the Koran was on his bedside table.**

Here is a more complete list of works that should be italicized (or underlined, if one must resort to that extremity):

- Book-length poems (note that most poems are not book length): *The Ring and the Book*
- Plays: *Salome*
- Operas: *Carmen*
- Movies: *The Kiss in the Tunnel*
- Pamphlets: *Distress in East London*
- Television programs (the title of an episode from a program would have quotation marks since it is shorter): *The Honeymooners*
- Works of art: *Mona Lisa*
- Long musical works (a CD title would be italicized; a song title from the CD would have quotation marks around it): *Greatest Love Songs of the Victorian Era*

- Magazines and newspapers (an article title from the magazine or newspaper would have quotation marks around it): *The Stratford Herald*
- Ships, aircraft, spacecraft, trains: *Titanic,* USS *Cole* (don't italicize the USS); *Spirit of St. Louis; Endeavor; Orient Express*

Keep in mind that articles (*a, an,* and *the*) are italicized (underlined) only when they are part of the actual title. For instance:

❧ **Mr. Fillmore saw an excellent production of** *The Phantom of the Opera.*

The is part of the title of the opera. On the other hand, one would write:

❧ **I would have to have more money than I do to take the** *Orient Express* **train.**

Orient Express is the name of the train; *the* is not part of its name.

Be careful to only apply italics (underlining) to punctuation (commas, periods, question marks, exclamation marks, and the like) if that punctuation is part of the title.

❧ **May screamed, "There's never been a better novel than** *Pride and Prejudice***!"**

The exclamation point and the ending quotation mark are not italicized, since they are not part of the title of the book.

Adding Emphasis

Consider the following sentences. See if one can tell the difference:

❧ "I'm *certain* I'm going to have to arrest you," the police chief said slyly.

❧ "I'm certain *I'm* going to have to arrest you," the police chief said slyly.

❧ "I'm certain I'm going to *have* to arrest you," the police chief said slyly.

❧ "I'm certain I'm going to have to arrest *you*," the police chief said slyly.

❧ "I'm certain I'm going to have to arrest you," the police chief said *slyly*.

In each of the five sentences, the only difference is in the words that are italicized. The use of italics tells the reader where emphasis should be placed. This helps the writer let the reader know the speech patterns being used, and it also helps the reader understand those patterns.

Be careful not to overuse italics (underlining) for emphasis, or one will lose the emphasis one wants to communicate. Consider this sentence:

❧ "Constable, the *culprit* is *Mr. Peddington*, not *me*. I wasn't *there* when the *theft* happened," Mr. Walton cried *sullenly* to the policeman.

With so many words italicized, the emphasis has lost its effectiveness.

Indicating a Different Context
Read the following sentence and see if it makes sense:

❧ The angry newspaper editor said to the young reporter, "You imbecile! You used robbery when you should have used burglary."

Indeed. Is the editor telling the reporter that he or she committed the wrong crime? No. If the writer had used italics, then the sentence would make better sense.

The rule is that when words, numbers, or letters are used outside of their normal context, they should be italicized (underlined). So the sentence should be written this way:

❧ **The angry newspaper editor said to the reporter, "You imbecile! You used *robbery* when you should have used *burglary.*"**

Written this way, the sentence shows that the reporter used the words *robbery* and *burglary* incorrectly in his or her story.

One should also apply this rule if one is reproducing a sound through a word (e.g., using a form of onomatopoeia), as in:

❧ ***Brrr!* I didn't know it was this cold outside.**

or

❧ **When Meredith dropped her new teapot on the floor, she cringed as it went *kerplunk* when it landed.**

Foreign Terms

One last use of italics (or underlining) is related to the previous one. This rule says one should italicize (or underline) a foreign word or phrase.

❧ **I was wavering about whether to go to the fair with my friends, but I decided *carpe diem.***

If a foreign word or phrase has become so widely used in English that there would not be any question of its meaning (such as per diem), there is no need to italicize it.

Ellipsis Points

When **ellipsis points or marks** (three spaced periods) are used, the reader knows that some material from a quotation has been omitted. Consider this sentence:

> *"Miss Mary Fielding left the dance early because Mr. Huntington did not attend and she had a terrible headache," said Miss Jordan.*

If one needed to quote that sentence, but out of delicacy did not wish to include the part about Mr. Huntington not attending (or if, perhaps, it had no relevance to one's point), one could use ellipsis points in this way:

> *"Miss Mary Fielding left the dance early because . . . she had a terrible headache," said Miss Jordan.*

Note that one should use ellipsis points only if the meaning of the sentence is not changed by what one omits. Consider this sentence:

> *The policeman reported, "The carriage involved in the accident had been stolen and then driven by a woman whom friends called 'Honest Harriet.'"*

One should not use ellipsis marks to shorten it this way:

> *The policeman reported, "The carriage involved in the accident had been . . . driven by a woman whom friends called 'Honest Harriet.'"*

In doing so, one would be leaving out some rather vital information.

If the material one is omitting occurs at the end of a sentence, or if one omits the last part of a quoted sentence but what is left remains grammatically complete, one would use four ellipsis points, with the first one functioning as a period. Take this original passage:

> ❧ *"A number of new people have joined the secret club. In fact, its membership has never been higher. Because the club is devoted to reading classical literature, however, its secret enrollment numbers have not been questioned by the public at large."*

One could use ellipsis marks in these ways:

> ❧ *"A number of new people have joined the secret club. . . . Because the club is devoted to reading classical literature, however, its secret enrollment numbers have not been questioned by the public at large."*

or

> ❧ *"A number of new people have joined. . . . [M]embership has never been higher. Because the club is devoted to reading classical literature, however, its secret enrollment numbers have not been questioned by the public at large."*

Another use for ellipsis marks is in quoting someone and trying to show that there is a deliberate pause in what the person said. Read the following paragraph:

> ❧ *James thought to himself, "If I can just hold on to the rail long enough for the train to reach New York, I know*

I can jump off. . . . I have to pace myself and keep watching the signs. . . . Twenty-five miles . . . Fifteen miles . . . Two miles . . . Done!"

The ellipsis marks tell one's readers that they are reading all of Jimmy's thoughts, with the marks indicating pauses between each individual thought.

The Slash/Virgule/Solidus

A **slash** (also called a *virgule* or a *solidus*) is commonly used to mean *or*. Thus:

- ❧ *slash/virgule/solidus = slash or virgule or solidus*

- ❧ *You may bring your spouse/sibling to the Winter Ball. = You may bring your spouse or sibling to the Winter Ball.*

Some other uses of the slash are:

1. In mathematics, the slash is used to mean *per*, as in this sentence:

- ❧ *There are 5,280 feet/mile.*

2. A slash is used to form fractions:

- ❧ *9/16 (meaning 9 divided by 16)*

3. In literature, the slash separates lines of poetry that are written in a block style, as in this passage from Edgar Allan Poe's "The Raven":

- ❧ *Once upon a midnight dreary, while I pondered, weak and weary, / Over many a quaint and curious volume of forgotten lore—/ While I nodded, nearly napping, suddenly there came a tapping, / As of some one gently rapping, rapping at my chamber door—/ " 'Tis some visitor," I muttered, "tapping at my chamber door—/ Only this and nothing more. . . ."*

4. With the popularity of the Internet, a common use of a slash is in URLs.

❧ *His home page is at <www.myownwebsite.com/ MarkPhillips/home>.*

Nota bene: Also note the use of angle brackets in the Internet address. This is one of the rare uses outside of mathematics for this symbol.

CHAPTER 7

WRITING BETTER SENTENCES

If a sentence contains a misplaced or dangling modifier or is essentially illogical, it becomes confusing at best and ludicrous at worst. Some brief sentences, called fragments, do not contain a complete thought and are not proper sentences at all. At the other extreme, a writer may sometimes string several thoughts together to create a hard-to-follow—and grammatically incorrect—run-on sentence.

The Author shudders to think that an author may unwittingly mangle the language in this manner. And yet it happens. Herein, one will find suggestions for ways in which one can examine one's sentence construction to determine if one has, indeed, made a fine mess. But that is not to say one will be abandoned to solve the problem oneself—nay! The Author will provide the tools one requires to fix any problems one encounters. Knowing what makes a proper sentence will ensure that one's writing (and one's reputation) remains beyond reproach.

Misplaced Modifiers

Simply put, **misplaced modifiers** are words or phrases that one has put in the wrong place. All modifiers should be placed as close as possible to whatever they describe or give more information about. Consider this sentence:

❧ *After being thrown from her horse, Joanna could comprehend what the doctor was barely saying.*

The way the sentence is written, the doctor is barely speaking—but surely that is not what the writer meant. *Barely* should be moved so that it modifies the verb *could comprehend.* The sentence should be written this way:

❧ *After being thrown from her horse, Joanna could barely comprehend what the doctor was saying.*

Misplaced modifiers can also be phrases, as in this example:

❧ *Witnesses reported that the woman rode away in a carriage with flowing black hair.*

A carriage with flowing black hair? That would be a truly astounding thing, were it true. *With flowing black hair* is in the wrong place and should be moved as follows:

❧ *Witnesses reported that the woman with flowing black hair rode away in a carriage.*

Clauses, too, can be put in the wrong place, as in the following sentence:

❧ *Mrs. Anderson could not stop thinking about her sick baby cleaning the kitchen floor.*

While it is never too young to train a child to work, it is quite probable that the author of this wretched sentence did not intend to imply that the baby was cleaning the kitchen floor. It has been The Author's experience that babies are much better at making messes on the kitchen floor than at cleaning them up, particularly when they are sick babies. The clause *cleaning the kitchen floor* should be closer to the noun it modifies (*Mrs. Anderson*). The sentence should be reworded this way:

❧ *Cleaning the kitchen floor, Mrs. Anderson could not stop thinking about her sick baby.*

One of the most common problems with misplaced modifiers comes with what are called limiting modifiers—words like *almost, even, hardly, just, merely, nearly, only* (*only* is the one misplaced most often), *scarcely,* and *simply.* To convey the correct meaning, limiting modifiers must be placed in front of the words they modify. Take a look at this sentence:

> ❧ **Richard has nearly ruined every book he has owned.**

Has Richard *nearly ruined* the books—in which case, he should be grateful for his luck—or has he ruined *nearly every book*? Watch out for misplaced modifiers (as Richard should probably watch out for spilled ink) to avoid ruining nearly every sentence one writes.

Dangling Modifiers

Dangling modifiers have no word or phrase to describe; they just dangle, or hang, in the sentence without something to hold on to. Consider these sentences:

> ❧ **Long ears drooping on the floor, Julia wondered how the dog could walk.**

Is it time for Julia to consider pinning her ears back?

> ❧ **While performing, the audience gasped as the singer forgot the words to the song.**

Why was the audience performing?

The above sentences need to be reworded so that the modifiers have something to attach to.

> ❧ **Julia wondered how the dog could walk with its long ears drooping on the floor.**
> ❧ **The audience gasped as the singer forgot the words to the song while he was performing.**

Squinting Modifiers

Squinting modifiers (sometimes called two-way modifiers) are words that can logically modify or describe something on either side of them, but the reader cannot be sure what the words modify. Consider this sentence:

> ❧ *The parson said after the ceremony ended that Mr. Wharton could kiss the bride.*

What does *after the ceremony ended* apply to? Did the parson *tell* Mr. Wharton this after the ceremony ended, or was Mr. Wharton *eligible* to kiss the bride after the ceremony ended? To correct this sentence, change the placement of the modifier:

> ❧ *After the ceremony ended, the parson said that Mr. Wharton was now allowed to kiss the bride.*

or

> ❧ *The parson said that Mr. Wharton was allowed to kiss the bride after the ceremony ended.*

Parallelism in Writing

Using **parallelism** means that one writes all the similar parts of a sentence in the same way. If one has used two nouns, one does not (or should not) suddenly switch to a gerund. If one has used verbs that have a certain tense, one does not suddenly change tenses.

Here are some of the rules for writing with parallel constructions.

1. When naming items, present them all in the same way. Consider this problem sentence:

❧ *This afternoon I cleared* [past tense verb with –ed], *dusted* [past tense verb with –ed], *and then I was polishing* [past progressive tense verb with –ing] *the dining room table.*

Here is the repaired sentence that is now parallel:

❧ *This afternoon I cleared, dusted, and polished the dining room table.*

2. When using more than one clause, keep the same voice and type of introduction in each. Here is the problem sentence:

❧ *Mrs. Cheltenham was worried that Mr. Cheltenham would spend too much money* [active voice], *that the bill would be too large* [active voice], *and the household would be bankrupted by the purchase of the new carriage* [passive voice].

To make the sentence parallel, the last clause can be changed to the active voice:

❧ *Mrs. Cheltenham was worried that Mr. Cheltenham would spend too much money, that the bill would be too large, and the that purchase of a new carriage would bankrupt the household.*

3. Place items in a series in similar locations. Consider this sentence:

❧ *The Frenchman is not only* [correlative conjunction *not only* comes after the verb] *very kind but also* [correlative conjunction *but also* comes before the verb] *is very good-looking.*

Here is the repaired sentence that is now parallel:

❧ *The Frenchman is not only very kind but also very good-looking.*

4. Order items in a series by chronology or degree of importance. Consider this problem sentence:

❧ *Misuse of laudanum can result in euphoria, death, or constipation.*

Now, identify the problem:

❧ *Misuse of laudanum can result in euphoria* [something that is, arguably, bad], *death* [something that is the worst of the three], *or constipation* [something that is bad].

Here is the repaired sentence that is now parallel:

❧ *Misuse of laudanum can result in euphoria, constipation, or death.*

In writing one's sentence this way, one builds up to the climax, to the worst problem—death. One could also include a word or phrase before the last element to add to the buildup, if one were inclined to be overly emotive:

❧ *Misuse of laudanum can result in euphoria, constipation, or even death.*

5. Use prepositions for items in a series consistently and correctly. Consider this problem sentence:

❧ *I hope to see you on November 20, December 13, and on January 7.*

Here, the preposition *on* occurs before the first and third items in the series. To be consistent, delete the *on* before *January 7*. The first *on* will then apply to all the items in the series.

If different prepositions apply to items in a series, be sure to include all the correct prepositions:

> ❧ *The invading ants are on the living room floor, the dining room table, and the sink.*

The preposition normally used before *the sink* would be *in*, not *on*. Here's the repaired sentence:

> ❧ *The invading ants are on the living room floor, on the dining room table, and in the sink.*

6. Sentences constructed in a parallel way are often more effective. Consider this example:

> ❧ *I was nervous and frightened, but I hid my emotions. My sister showed the world that she felt confident and carefree.*

There is no grammatical mistake with the sentences, but they can certainly be improved by being written in a parallel manner, as below:

> ❧ *I was nervous and frightened, but I hid my emotions. My sister was confident and carefree, but she showed the world how she felt.*

Writing Logically

No matter how meticulous one is in crafting the grammar and punctuation of one's sentences, if one's material has errors in logic, all of one's hard work will have been for naught. As one writes, keep the following common mistakes in mind—and do not make them!

1. **Faulty predication** occurs when the subject and verb do not make sense together (that is, the subject cannot "be" or "do" the verb). Take a look at these sentences:

❧ *Mr. Sikeston is a tooth that is bothering him.*

❧ *The new tonic assures customers that it will cure everything from pneumonia to the plague.*

Obviously, Mr. Sikeston isn't a tooth (unless one names one's teeth), and a tonic is incapable of assuring anybody of anything. Each of these sentences needs to be reworded, perhaps like this:

❧ *Mr. Sikeston has a tooth that is bothering him.*

❧ *The makers of the new tonic assure customers that it will cure everything from pneumonia to the plague.*

2. **Faulty coordination** occurs if one joins (combines or coordinates) two clauses in an illogical way:

❧ *I made my way into the butcher's shop, yet I realized I had forgotten my money.*

The word *yet* is used incorrectly. The sentence should read:

❧ *I made my way into the butcher's shop, but then I realized I had forgotten my money.*

Another example of faulty coordination comes in sentences that contain independent clauses of unequal importance, as in the following sentence:

❧ *The Vanderbilts paid $50,000 for an evening's entertainment; it included swans.*

The cost of the event is more important than the fact that it had swans. To correct the problem, one could make the second clause subordinate to the first.

❧ *The Vanderbilts paid $50,000 for an evening's entertainment, which included swans.*

3. **Absolute adjectives** are words that cannot be compared. *Vacant*, for instance—something is either vacant or it is not.
   Other absolute adjectives include the following:

   eternal
   favorite
   permanent
   unanimous
   unique

   Consider this example:

❧ *Miss Hampton-Reed spent the afternoon napping rather than writing letters; the stationery at her elbow was somewhat blank.*

One cannot have a paper that is somewhat blank; either it has something on it or it does not. Since these are words that cannot be compared, be sure not to use *more, most, quite, rather, somewhat, very,* and other qualifiers in front of them.

4. **Faulty comparison** occurs if one compares two unlike people, places, or things:

❧ *The party invitations in April were more numerous than May.*

This sentence compares invitations to May, which makes no sense. The sentence should be rewritten like this:

❧ *The party invitations in April were more numerous than the invitations in May.*

Another problem is an ambiguous comparison that could be interpreted two different ways. Consider this sentence:

❧ *Mr. Penniworth dislikes traveling alone more than Mrs. Penniworth.*

The reader is not sure what the word *more* applies to. Does Mr. Penniworth dislike traveling alone more than he dislikes his wife, or does he dislike traveling alone more than she dislikes traveling alone?

5. **Sweeping (or hasty) generalizations** use all-encompassing words like *anyone, everyone, always, never, everything, all, only,* and *none,* and superlatives like *best, greatest, most, least.*

❧ *If one is fired from a position, one can never find a new one at the same rate of pay.*

Be careful with sentences with gener-alizations like this one. What happens to one's credibility if a worker does, in fact, find a new position at the same rate of pay? One possible rewording of the example is this:

❧ *If one is fired from a position, one can almost never find a new one at the same rate of pay.*

6. **A non sequitur** states an effect that fails to logically follow from its cause.

❧ *Mr. Darcy asked Miss Bennet to marry him; therefore, she will.*

As Mr. Darcy will concede, asking a woman for her hand in marriage does not mean she will consent. What if she has plighted her troth to another? Or despises the man who asks? One should only begin planning the wedding after the bride-to-be says yes.

7. One frequent mistake in logic comes from **omitting necessary words in comparisons**. Read this sentence:

🖎 *Aunt Lucy likes Cousin Louise more than she likes anyone in the family.*

The way the sentence is written, Cousin Louise is not in the family. The sentence needs to be reworded this way:

🖎 *Aunt Lucy likes Cousin Louise more than she likes anyone else in the family.*

Sometimes sentences need the word *than* or *as* in order for them to be logical:

🖎 *Miss Primpton said she could play the pianoforte as well, if not better than, Miss Evesham.*

Taking out the phrase *if not better than* leaves the illogical statement *Miss Primpton said she could play the pianoforte as well Miss Evesham.* The sentence should be written with the extra *as* to complete the phrase:

🖎 *Miss Primpton said she could play the pianoforte as well as, if not better than, Miss Evesham.*

8. Another mistake in logic is commonly called ***post hoc, ergo propter hoc,*** which translates as *after this, so because of this.* Here the assumption is that because one thing follows another, the first caused the second.

🖎 *Because Mr. Felix shook his fist at the sky, it started to thunder and lightning.*

9. Other errors of logic include:

- A **false dilemma** (sometimes called an either/or fallacy) states that only two alternatives exist, when there are actually more than two:

🖐 *Mrs. Robertson can get to her appointment in one of two ways: She can either drive her carriage or she can walk.* **(Mrs. Robertson has other choices: She could call a hack or ask a friend for a ride.)**

- A **red herring** dodges the real issue by citing an irrelevant concern as evidence:

🖐 *Miss Simpre can eat all the clotted cream she likes and never breaks out in spots; How am I ever going to catch Mr. Widdlesworth's eye?* **(Miss Simpre's luck doesn't have anything to do with the speaker's dilemma.)**

- **Circular reasoning** goes around in a circle (naturally), with nothing substantial in the middle. Here is an example:

🖐 *The epidemic was dangerous because everyone in town felt unsafe and at risk.* **(The second part of the sentence provides no clarification about why the epidemic was dangerous.)**

Sentence Fragments

A sentence fragment is not, by definition, actually a sentence. A sentence, one may recall from Chapter 3, is a group of words that (1) has a subject, (2) has a predicate (verb), and (3) expresses a complete thought.

If a string of words does not have all three of the qualifications, then one is in possession of a fragment rather than a sentence. Consider these two words:

❧ *Spot ran.*

One has a subject (*Spot*), a verb (*ran*), and the words express a complete thought. Because all of the elements are present and accounted for, these two words form a complete sentence.

Now, consider this group of words:

❧ *Although she had a litter of kittens in the barn.*

This example is a subordinate clause that is punctuated as if it were a sentence, yet it is a fragment! It certainly has a subject (*she*) and indeed a verb (*had*), but what it does not have is a complete thought. The sentence below is one example of how this thought could be completed:

❧ *Although she had a litter of kittens in the barn, the mama cat ignored them.*

A participial phrase often creates another common sentence fragment, as below:

❧ *Scared stiff by the intense wind and storm.*

Who was scared stiff? Obviously, something is missing. Read the following paragraph and try to spot the fragments:

❧ *The lone woman trudged up the muddy riverbank. Determined that she would make the best of a bad situation. Because of her family's recent run of bad luck. She knew that she had to contribute to the family's finances. That's why she had accepted a teaching position. In this town that was new to her. Impatiently waiting for someone to show her where she was to live. She surveyed the streets and rundown buildings of the little village. The schoolhouse was not ready. Even though she had written that she wanted to begin classes on the 24th. The day after her arrival.*

How many fragments are there?

- *Determined that she would make the best of a bad situation.*
- *Because of her family's recent run of bad luck.*
- *In this town that was new to her.*
- *Impatiently waiting for someone to show her where she was to live.*
- *Even though she had written that she wanted to begin classes on the 24th.*
- *The day after her arrival.*

If one had those words alone on a piece of paper, would anybody know what one meant? No—those words do not form complete thoughts.

Now, how can one correct these fragments? Usually the fragment should be connected to the sentence immediately before or after it—whichever sentence the fragment refers to. (A word of caution: be certain that the newly created sentence makes sense.)

Here is one way one could correct the paragraph to eliminate the fragments:

- *Determined that she would make the best of a bad situation, the lone woman trudged up the muddy riverbank. She knew that, because of her family's recent run of bad luck, she had to contribute to the family's finances. As she waited impatiently for someone to show her where she was to live, she surveyed the village. The schoolhouse was not ready, even though she had written that she wanted to begin classes on the 24th, the day after her arrival.*

Note that to add variety to the paragraph, some fragments have been added to beginning of other sentences some to the end, and one (*because of her family's recent run of bad luck*) was inserted in the middle of a sentence.

Fragments should never be used in formal writing however, using them occasionally is acceptable for a casual writing style, such as when one is leaving a note for the cook. Using fragments (even sparingly) depends on one's audience and one's personal writing style. Acceptable uses of a fragment include the following:

- In a short story or novel (but not excessively)
- When quoting someone else
- In a bulleted or numbered list (such this one)
- To make a quick point—but only when the construction is not confusing to the reader

Run-on Sentences

Another mistaken sentence construction is a **run-on sentence**. The term *run-on* means that one's sentence, like Great-Aunt Mildred, goes on and on without stopping. To be specific, it has at least two complete thoughts (two independent clauses, that is), but it lacks the necessary punctuation between the thoughts.

One type of run-on, called a **fused sentence**, occurs when two (or more) sentences are fused together without a punctuation mark to show the reader where the break occurs. Consider this sentence:

❧ *For the picnic, Mr. and Mrs. Poole brought champagne we brought roast chicken.*

In the sentence, there are two separate thoughts: *For the picnic, Mr. and Mrs. Poole brought champagne* and *we brought roast chicken.*

To make clear where one thought ends and another begins, one can:

❧ **Create two separate sentences:** *For the picnic, Mr. and Mrs. Poole brought champagne. We brought roast chicken.*

❧ **Insert a semicolon:** *For the picnic, Mr. and Mrs. Poole brought champagne; we brought roast chicken.*

❧ **Insert a comma and one of seven conjunctions—but, or, yet, so, for, and, nor:** *For the picnic, Mr. and Mrs. Poole brought champagne, and we brought roast chicken.*

Another type of run-on is a **comma splice** (sometimes known as a comma fault), a sentence that has two complete thoughts that are spliced together by just a comma. Consider this sentence:

❧ *Mr. Masington wanted to go to the opera, his friend Mr. Witley wanted to see the cabaret.*

On either side of the comma, one has a complete thought. Because a sentence is a complete thought, they cannot be joined together with a comma. They must be separated into separate sentences, joined with a semicolon, or combined by adding a conjunction, as with the fused sentence above:

❧ *Mr. Masington wanted to go to the opera. His friend Mr. Witley wanted to see the cabaret* [using a period].

❧ *Mr. Masington wanted to go to the opera; his friend Mr. Witley wanted to see the cabaret* [using a semicolon].

🔖 *Mr. Masington wanted to go to the opera, but his friend Mr. Witley wanted to see the cabaret* [using a comma and conjunction].

Another way to correct either a fused sentence or a comma splice is to reword the sentence so that one part becomes subordinate to the other. Consider the first example:

🔖 *For the picnic, Mr. and Mrs. Poole brought champagne we brought roast chicken.*

One might reword the sentence in this way:

🔖 *For the picnic, while Mr. and Mrs. Poole brought champagne, we brought roast chicken.*

Transitional Words and Phrases

Good writers rely on the use of **transitional words and phrases** (one might be more familiar with the terms *connecting words* or *parenthetical expressions*). Transitional words and phrases show one's readers the association between thoughts, sentences, or paragraphs, and they help make one's writing smoother. Consider the following paragraph:

🔖 *The call was a disaster. It was a complete debacle. I was intrigued by what my friend Sarah had told me about her cousin, Mr. Hightower; she had said that he was charming and had seen me at a party and had asked if she thought it would be all right to call on me. Sarah said Mr. Hightower was a perfect match. She said that he was an avid reader; we would have lots to talk about. He liked playing croquet; that was a plus for me. I agreed to accept a call from Mr. Hightower.*

There is nothing wrong with the grammar, punctuation, or spelling in that paragraph, but it is choppy and boring. Now read the same paragraph after transitional words and phrases (underlined) have been added:

❧ *The call was <u>more than</u> a disaster. <u>In fact</u>, it was a complete debacle. <u>At first</u>, I was intrigued by what my friend Sarah had told me about her cousin, Mr. Hightower; <u>namely</u>, she had said that he was charming and that he had recently seen me <u>in the distance</u> at a party and had asked if it would be all right to call on me. <u>Besides</u>, Sarah said, Mr. Hightower was a perfect match. <u>For one thing</u>, she said that he was an avid reader; <u>therefore</u>, we would have lots to talk about. <u>In addition</u>, he liked playing croquet; that was a plus for me. <u>So</u>, I <u>eventually</u> agreed to accept a call from Mr. Hightower <u>on Saturday</u>.*

By including the transitions, the movement from one idea to another is much smoother, and the language of the paragraph has some life in it.

Classifying the Connectors

Transitional words and phrases can be divided into categories according to their use. The following should give ideas for adding transitional elements to one's writing:

- addition/sequence: *additionally, afterward, again, also, and, and then, another, besides, equally important, eventually, finally, first . . . second . . . third, further, furthermore, in addition, in the first place, initially, last, later, likewise, meanwhile, moreover, next, other, overall, second, still, third, too, what's more*

- concession: *admittedly, although it is true that, certainly, conceding that, granted that, in fact, it may appear that, naturally, no doubt, of course, surely, undoubtedly, without a doubt*
- contrast: *after all, alternatively, although, and yet, at the same time, but, conversely, despite, even so, even though, for all that, however, in contrast, in spite of, instead, nevertheless, nonetheless, nor, notwithstanding, on the contrary, on the other hand, or, otherwise, regardless, still, though, yet*
- examples, clarification, emphasis: *after all, an instance of this, as an illustration, by all means, certainly, clearly, definitely, e.g., even, for example, for instance, for one thing, i.e., importantly, indeed, in fact, in other words, in particular, in short, more than that, namely, of course, of major concern, once again, somewhat, specifically, such as, that is, that is to say, the following example, this can be seen in, thus, to clarify, to demonstrate, to illustrate, to put another way, to repeat, to rephrase, truly, undoubtedly, without a doubt*
- place or direction: *above, adjacent to, at that point, below, beyond, close by, closer to, elsewhere, far, farther on, here, in the back, in the distance, in the front, near, nearby, neighboring on, next to, on the other side, opposite to, overhead, there, to the left, to the right, to the side, under, underneath, wherever*
- purpose/cause and effect: *accordingly, as a consequence, as a result, because, consequently, due to, for that reason, for this purpose, hence, in order that, on account of, since, so, so that, then, therefore, thereupon, thus, to do this, to this end, with this in mind, with this objective*
- qualification: *almost, although, always, frequently, habitually, maybe, nearly, never, often, oftentimes, perhaps, probably, time and again*
- result: *accordingly, and so, as a result, as an outcome, consequently, hence, so, then, therefore, thereupon, thus*
- similarity: *again, also, and, as well as, besides, by the same token, for example, furthermore, in a like manner, in a similar*

way, in the same way, like, likewise, moreover, once more, similarly, so

- summary or conclusion: *after all, all in all, as a result, as has been noted, as I have said, as we have seen, as mentioned earlier, as stated, clearly, finally, in any event, in brief, in conclusion, in other words, in particular, in short, in simpler terms, in summary, on the whole, that is, therefore, to conclude, to summarize*

- time: *after a bit, after a few days, after a while, afterward, again, also, and then, as long as, as soon as, at first, at last, at length, at that time, at the same time, before, during, earlier, eventually, finally, first, following, formerly, further, hence, initially, immediately, in a few days, in the first place, in the future, in the meantime, in the past, last, lately, later, meanwhile, next, now, on (a certain day), once, presently, previously, recently, second, shortly, simultaneously, since, so far, soon, still, subsequently, then, thereafter, this time, today, tomorrow, until, until now, when, whenever*

CHAPTER 8
AVOIDING COMMON ERRORS

This chapter includes an overview of some common grammatical and stylistic errors that writers commonly commit, along with tips for avoiding them in one's writing. The Author will discuss, as clearly, concisely, and elegantly as always, how to rid one's writing of clichés, redundancies, wordiness, and the dreaded double negative as well as how to overcome other avoidable writing and style errors. If, at the close of this chapter, one has not learned to stop using ten words when two will do, there is nothing The Author can do about it, and advises one to hire an editor.

Steering Clear of Clichés

A **cliché** is a worn-out expression, one that has been used over and over. In general, one should avoid using clichés because they are unoriginal, stale, and monotonous. Some examples:

costs an arm and a leg

every cloud has a silver lining

put all your eggs in one basket

read the handwriting on the wall

that's the way the cookie crumbles

there's more there than meets the eye

To reword any cliché that makes its way into one's writing, try "translating" it to say precisely what one means. For instance, suppose one has written this atrocity:

❧ *It was as plain as the nose on his face that Mr. Drew would not stick his neck out for anybody else.*

In that sentence, one is dealing with two clichés *(plain as the nose on his face* and *stick his neck out)*. To make the sentence cliché free, one could change it to:

🖋 *Plainly, Mr. Drew would not take a risk for anybody else.*

Eliminating Repetition

When it comes to writing, **redundant words or phrases** not only diminish the value of the work but also waste the reader's time. Here are some examples of some common redundant phrases, along with explanations of why they are redundant.

COMMON REDUNDANT PHRASES	
REDUNDANT PHRASE	**EXPLANATION**
advance planning	Planning is always done in advance.
A.M. in the morning	If occurring in the morning, it has to be A.M.
and also	Use one word or the other; not both.
ask the question	It is impossible to ask anything except a question.
assembled together	It is impossible to assemble apart. Delete *together.*
cash money	Is cash ever anything but money?
combined together	Things that are combined must be together. Delete *together.*
each and every	The words mean the same thing; delete one.
fewer in number	As opposed to fewer in what else?
green in color	As opposed to green in what?
large in size	The word *large* denotes size; use *large* only.
may possibly	If something may happen, it is possible to happen.
mix together	It is impossible to mix apart, is it not?
rectangular in shape	If something is rectangular, that is its shape.
same identical	Something that is identical must be the same. Delete one word or the other.
sum total	If one has a sum, one has a total. Delete one word or the other.
unexpected surprise	If a surprise is expected, it is not a surprise.

Cutting Out Wordy Expressions

Wordiness is the first cousin of redundant writing. Take a look at the following list of common wordy expressions, then get to work putting one's own prose on a diet.

SUGGESTED SUBSTITUTES FOR WORDY PHRASES

WORDY PHRASE	SUGGESTED SUBSTITUTE
a considerable number of	many
a number of	some, several
adverse impact on	hurt, set back
affords the opportunity of	allows, lets
along the lines of	like
am of the opinion	think
are of the same opinion	agree
arrived at the conclusion	concluded
as a consequence	because
as a matter of fact	in fact
as a means of	to
ascertain the location of	find
at the present time	currently, now, today
at this point in time	now
based on the fact that	because
be aware of the fact that	know
came to a realization	realized
come to an agreement	agree
concerning the matter of	about, regarding
conduct an investigation (or) experiment	investigate, experiment
considering the fact that	because, since
despite the fact that	although, though
draw to your attention	show, point out
each and every one	each, all
extend an invitation to	invite
for the reason that	because, since, why

give an indication of	show
has a requirement for	requires, needs
has the ability to, has the capacity for	can
if conditions are such that	if
in a position to	can, may, will
in addition to	besides, beyond, and, plus
in all likelihood (or) probability	likely, probably
in an effort to	to
in close proximity to	near, close, about
in large measure	largely
in light of the fact that	since, because
in spite of the fact that	although, despite
in the absence of	without
in the course of	during, while, in, at
in the event of (or) that	if
in the final analysis	finally
in the majority of instances	usually
in the midst of	during, amid
in the neighborhood of	near, close, about
in the very near future	soon
in this day and age	currently, now, today
in view of the fact that	because, since
is aware of the fact that	knows
it is imperative that we	we must
it is my understanding	I understand
it is often the case that	often
make a decision	decide
make a purchase	buy
make an application	apply
make an inquiry regarding	ask about, inquire about
notwithstanding the fact that	although
on the grounds that	because, since, why
one of the	a, an, one
owing to the fact that	because, since, why

place a major emphasis on	stress
take into consideration	consider
that being the case	therefore
the fact that	that
through the use of	through, by, with
to a certain degree	somewhat
under circumstances in which	when

Double Negatives

Now for the **double negative**; that is, two negative words that are used to stress denial or opposition. Examples of these include:

❧ *After he was fired from the mill, Mr. Brown realized that he didn't need none of the luxuries he had become accustomed to.*

(*Didn't* and *none* are negatives.)

❧ *That man was not doing nothing but just standing there!*

(*Not* and *nothing* are negatives.)

The way to correct a double negative is generally to change one of the negative expressions. For example, in the first example above, change *none* to *any*:

❧ *After he was fired from the mill, Mr. Brown realized that he didn't need any of the luxuries he'd become accustomed to.*

One exception to the rule of avoiding double negatives is when one intends a positive or lukewarm meaning. Consider this sentence:

🖎 *She was not unhappy with her choice of dress.*

The connotation in the double negatives *(not* and *unhappy)* tells the reader that, while the writer was not unhappy, she was not exactly in a swoon either.

It is also fine to use double negatives if one is using a phrase or clause for emphasis, as in this example:

🖎 *"I will not take a bribe, not today, not tomorrow, not any time in my life," the politician cried.*

CONCLUSION

Dear reader, one has now learned all that The Author can teach one about grammar and usage. Now one must put the lessons to use so that one's words are met with the approbation they deserve rather than the ridicule they do not. Herewith are The Author's final thoughts about writing well:

1. **Read one's work out loud.** Before one submits one's work to another's scrutiny, one must read it out loud to oneself, or, if he or she is available, to one's Maltese. Out loud, one must read more slowly, so one will often catch grammatical and spelling mistakes and similar constructions that one would miss in silent reading. However, do not expect the Maltese to aid with the writing process. Rather, the Maltese is there so that one does not look like a fool for talking to oneself.

2. **Read backward.** Start at the end and read the last sentence, then the sentence before that, and so on until one reaches the beginning. When one reads out of order, one will more easily spot errors.

3. **Look for one's most frequent past errors.** As the Roman poet Juvenal commanded, "Know thyself." If, for instance, one has trouble with sentence fragments, go back through one's work and closely examine each sentence to make certain that it is a whole, complete, and entire sentence.

4. **Check one's spelling oneself.** A spell checker will detect only words that are not in the dictionary. A good idea is to make one pass through one's copy looking for spelling errors alone.

5. **Check one's tense usage.** If one began one's piece using the past tense, for example, make sure that one has written the rest in the past tense as well (not including any quoted material, of course).

6. **Let someone else proofread and respond to one's work.** This is where having dependents can play a practical role, as they cannot very easily refuse one's request. Ask the other readers to be as critical as possible and to look for any kind of error—in spelling, punctuation, usage, mechanics, organization, clarity, even in the value of one's ideas. Chances are if he or she had trouble reading or understanding one's material, one should do some extra revision.

INDEX